TEENAGERS AND THE CHURCH

TEENAGERS AND THE CHURCH

A profile of church-going youth in the 1980's

Leslie J. Francis

Research Officer, Culham College Institute for Church Related Education

Collins

Collins Liturgical Publications
187 Piccadilly, London W1V 9DA

Collins Liturgical Australia
P.O. Box 3023, Sydney 2001

© 1984 Leslie J. Francis
ISBN 0 00 599773 9
First published 1984

Data capture by Culham College Institute for Church Related Education
Phototypeset by Burgess & Son (Abingdon) Ltd
Printed in Great Britain by Richard Clay (The Chaucer Press) Ltd,
Bungay, Suffolk

CONTENTS

FOREWORD

This study of teenagers and the church had its origin in a working party set up by the British Council of Churches in 1979. The working party identified the need for a fresh research initiative into the teenagers who have contact with the churches. The opportunity to establish a research project into this issue came from co-operation between the British Council of Churches Youth Unit, S. Martin's College Lancaster, and the Lancashire Council for Ecumenical Youth Work. The first results of this project were included in the working party report, published by the British Council of Churches in 1981, under the title *Young People and the Church*.

As honorary research director of the project, I inherited the data and undertook the task of completing a full and thorough analysis. I believe that this analysis provides the churches with a whole set of unique insights into the beliefs, attitudes, values and practices of the teenagers with whom they have contact.

Many churches find it hard to keep in touch with teenagers: between the ages of thirteen and twenty a number of young people drift away. But who are the teenagers who remain in touch with the churches? Why do they keep going? What do they look for from the churches, and how satisfied are they with what they find? What can the churches learn from the teenagers whom they continue to attract? The present study sets out to discover the answers to these questions by analysing the replies of over thirteen hundred church-going teenagers.

The writing of this book has enabled me to bring together my two professional concerns, my concern as a social psychologist with attitude measurement and my concern as a parish priest with the place of young people in the church. My aim in writing has been to communicate the insights generated from serious social research to those who are not themselves social researchers. For this reason I have tended to avoid an excess of technical language. Similarly, I have kept statistical tables to a minimum and placed them in an appendix.

In preparing the data for this study, full use has been made of the statistical tests of significance, factor analysis, multiple regression, analysis of variance, tests of linearity, and so on, which characterise my papers in the scientific journals. However, I decided that this was not the kind of book in which it would be either necessary or helpful to report this level of methodological detail. The data bank is rich, and I hope that, having provided the churches with an overview of the main findings of the study, I shall be able at a later stage to return to the data to write in a more detailed way about the thorough exploration of certain issues of particular theoretical or methodological concern.

The range of issues covered in this book enables the views of these thirteen hundred thirteen to twenty year olds to be set alongside and compared with the views of the one thousand sixteen to twenty-five year olds and the two thousand twenty-six to thirty-nine year olds in my two earlier studies of the relationship between religion and social attitudes. These two studies, *Youth in Transit* and *Experience of Adulthood*, based on the membership of London Central YMCA, were both published by Gower in 1982.

The history of the present study of teenage church-goers means that I am deeply indebted to a number of individuals who contributed in many ways to the design and development of the research project. Serving on the working party were Michael Butterfield (chief executive, National Association of Youth Clubs), Helen Alexander (field officer, British Council of Churches Youth Unit), Tom Allen (youth adviser, Church Missionary Society), Richard Basch (research officer, S. Martin's College, Lancaster), John Bell (youth adviser, Church of Scotland), Murdoch Dahl (formerly Canon Theologian, St. Albans), Leslie Francis (research fellow, London Central YMCA), Debbie Hewitt (London weekend co-ordinator, Methodist Association of Youth Clubs), Carl Kuusk (theological student, St. John's College, Durham), Alan Lowe (principal youth and community officer, Dudley), John Parr (head of community and youth work department, Westhill College, Birmingham), David Pendle (Methodist Division of Education and Youth), Natasha Schemanoff (diocesan youth officer, St. Edmundsbury and Ipswich) and Michael Doe (youth secretary, British Council of Churches). Serving on the research advisory group were Andy Smith, Chris Williams and Richard Basch (the three representatives from S. Martin's College, Lancaster), Bernard Grimsey and Keith Knight (the two representatives from the Lancashire Council for Ecumenical Youth Work) and Michael Doe and Leslie Francis (the two representatives from the British Council of Churches Youth Unit working party).

Research of this nature is an expensive undertaking which would not have been possible without the financial support of several bodies. The working party was funded by the King George Jubilee Trust and the

National Christian Education Council. The research project was funded by the Department of Education and Science and S. Martin's College, Lancaster.

Finally, my special gratitude must go to Michael Doe, who pioneered the whole concept of undertaking the research project; to Richard Basch, who was responsible not only for collecting and organising the data, but also for preparing the initial report of the results; to my employers, formerly London Central YMCA and currently the Culham College Institute, who both encouraged me in undertaking and completing the work; to Sue Chapman and Nicola Slee who helped in the design and preparation of the text; to Heather Knight and Clare Gowing, who prepared the manuscript for printing; and to Judith Muskett for assistance with proof reading.

Culham College Institute,   Leslie J. Francis
July, 1983.

1 INTRODUCTION

One Sunday attend a service in a church or chapel where you are unknown and take a good look at the faces in the congregation. Try to guess the age of each of the worshippers. The older teenagers may well be noticeable by their absence.

Walk into a comprehensive school on Monday morning and try to discover how many of the pupils went to church the previous day. As you go up through the school from the first year to the fifth, so you will find the percentage of church-goers decreases. By the time of the school leaving age, very few young people would still be claiming allegiance to the Christian churches.

Attend an ecumencial conference and listen to the priests, clergy and ministers of religion from a variety of different denominations discuss the aspects of their ministry which cause them most anxiety. Not far below the surface of their immediate concerns you will find the problem of work among teenagers. The churches have enough difficulty in making contact with those in the pre-teenage years, and yet their work among younger children looks like a story of success when compared with their work among teenagers. The sadness for the minister is to recognise how the child once regular at Sunday school or faithful at children's services fails to grow into a teenage church attender, taking his or her place alongside the adult members of the worshipping community.

Attach yourself to a group of parents in a local church and talk to them about the religious development of their children. Parents who brought their pre-teenage children to service with them week by week will relate with sadness how the teenage child suddenly chooses a different way to spend his or her Sunday.

Think back to the teenage years, to the trauma and uncertainty of growing up, to the discontent with being a child and to the inability to become an adult. Recall how easy it is to understand the rebellion of this age group as they try to assert their independence, from parents, from school, from church. At the same time, consider the lack of resources which the churches in your own neighbourhood have for making an adequate attempt to communicate with the teenager. Review what these churches have available in terms of buildings, activities and trained personnel to meet the special needs of the teenage years. Is it surprising that such a large gap exists between teenagers and the church today?

The general absence of teenagers from the churches makes those who are church attenders of great interest and importance to the churches. Who are the teenagers who remain in touch with the churches? Why do they keep going? What do they look for from the churches, and how satisfied are they with what they find? What can the churches learn from the teenagers whom they continue to attract?

It was questions like these which stimulated the establishment of the present research project, and which the present book sets out to answer. Having posed the basic questions, my aim in this introduction is to explain how the book is organised and to provide the reader with a guide to its use.

Before the usefulness of the results of a research project can be assessed, it is wise to look in some detail at the methods used to collect the information. After all, a research project stands or falls by the credentials of its methodology. Chapter 2, therefore, 'Research Design', looks in detail at the way in which the research was carried out. This involves looking at six related issues. What precisely does the research project set out to do? Why did I choose to collect the information by means of a self completion questionnaire, rather than by another method? How in fact was the questionnaire designed, and how reliable and valid is it? In what part of the country was the project located, and why? How were the churches selected to take part in this study, and what was their response like? How did we make contact with the teenagers themselves, and how well did they co-operate with the project?

Chapter 3, 'Teenage Church-goers', describes in detail the young people who took part in the survey. First, we want to know as much as possible about their background and who they are. What churches do they represent? What is the ratio between boys and girls among the teenage church-goers? How many thirteen year olds are there in church for every twenty year old church-goer? What kinds of schools have these young people attended? How many of them are still at school, and what are those who have left school now doing? What is their social background, and so on?

Second, we want to know what kind of involvement these young people actually have with their church. How many of them attend service every Sunday, and how many of them are more casual attenders? What kind of services do they attend? With whom do they go to church? Do they look to their families for support, or do they prefer to go with friends of their own age? At what age are these young people admitted to full membership of their church, and what kind of preparation do they receive before such admission? What kind of church activities do they support apart from Sunday services?

Chapter 4, 'Church Membership', examines what it means to teenage church-goers to belong to a local church. Specifically, this chapter focuses on four aspects of their church membership. First, we study the activities which teenagers undertake in the church and the activities which they would like to undertake. Second, we review the responsibilities which teenagers are given in the life of their local church, and the responsibilities which they would be willing to undertake. Third, we examine the topics which teenagers have the opportunity to discuss when they attend church groups, and the topics which they feel should be more generally and openly discussed in their church. Finally, we turn attention to the priorities which the teenagers feel should count in their local church. If teenagers were able to influence the programme of their local church, would they want to see more weight given to a social gospel, a spiritual gospel, a political gospel, or what?

Chapter 5, 'Public Worship', listens to what the teenage church-goers are saying about their attitudes to the public worship offered in their churches. Are they happy about what their local church is doing in its public services? Do they feel that these services are likely to attract other young people, and, if not, why not? How do they feel about change in worship? Do they prefer the traditional liturgy or modern forms of service? How do they feel about the clergy in their churches? Are they able to communicate with their clergy, or do they feel that there are insuperable barriers between the clergy and young people? And, finally, how do they relate to the older people in the church congregation? Is there a conflict between the generations, or not?

Chapter 6, 'Religious Beliefs', examines the relationship between public church attendance and personal religious belief and practice. How much priority do these teenagers who go to church on a Sunday give to their religion in their daily lives? Do they pray, read the bible, and so on? On what do they base their allegiance to a Christian church? How many of them trace their commitment to some personal experience of God? How many of them are familiar with the beliefs and practices of a range of Christian denominations or the other major world faiths? What in fact do they believe about God, about Jesus, about the resurrection and so on?

Chapter 7, 'Moral Attitudes', looks at the extent to which the religious beliefs of the teenage church-goers are projected onto the moral sphere. What are their views on sexuality, issues like sex outside marriage, homosexuality and contraception? What are their attitudes towards drugs and towards drink? What do they believe about the morality of euthanasia, abortion and war? How do they feel about the prevailing moral climate of the society in which they live? How do they regard society's attitude towards such issues as divorce, pornography and violence? How strictly do they keep the law, even when they feel that they can break it without being caught? How do they rate their own personal integrity?

Chapter 8, 'Politics and Society', assesses the involvement of the young church-goers in politics. How politically aware are they, and how passionately do they feel about the issues on which the major political parties hold opposing views? How socially aware are they, and how much do they care about the problems that confront their society and today's world?

Chapter 9, 'Work and Leisure', gives attention to the wider context in which the young church-goers live their lives. How content are they with their work, whether this means school, college or employment? How ambitious are they with their work? And how does their church membership relate to their working life? How content are they with their leisure time? What kind of leisure activities do they pursue? What proportion of the young church-goers are likely to be coming to church because they have nothing else to do, and what proportion are likely to be giving their church membership a high priority within a busy and fully occupied life?

Chapter 10, 'Well-being and Worry', turns attention to the psychological welfare of the young church-goers. Overall, how happy are they with their lives? What are their anxieties and worries? How much help do they feel that they need in coming to terms with life? Does belonging to a church help them at all?

The purpose of chapters 1–10 has been to make generalisations about teenage church-goers as a group. These chapters set out to compare the responses of the boys and girls, to discuss how their responses change as they grow older, and to examine whether the denominational groups differ much from each other. This kind of analysis has a central part to play in our attempt to understand the relationship between teenagers and the church today. However, this kind of analysis can only partially exhaust the wealth of information made available from the present survey.

After the previous chapters have accomplished the proper task of generalisations, Chapter 11, 'Character Sketches', turns attention to just a handful of the young people who attend church and draws in some detail their personal profiles. Space would never permit thirteen hundred detailed character studies, but a few case studies can serve to illustrate the richness of the data and remind us that, beneath the useful generalisations, we are the whole time dealing with uniqueness and individuality. In the last analysis, one of the greatest benefits of sociological generalisations about young people is the way in which these generalisations help us to gain insight into the individuals whom we know and among whom we work.

Finally, Chapter 12, 'Discussion', turns the work of the project away from the researcher and back to the local churches and to all of us who have a concern for the church's work among young people. I have not written a chapter of summary or set out my own personal conclusions. The issues at stake are too important for such treatment. Instead, I have articulated the questions which each chapter raises in my own mind and which I believe local churches would be wise to discuss and to study.

I hope that this final chapter will become the basis through which local churches will be able to assess their own work among teenagers and plan realistically for their future work. If the research project achieves this, many of the hopes of the working party which first initiated it will have been realised.

2 RESEARCH DESIGN

Before examining what the research project discovered about the teenagers who go to church, it is necessary to look in some detail at the methods used to collect this information. After all, the value of a research project must be assessed according to the credentials of its methodology. The purpose of this chapter, therefore, is to look in detail at the way in which the research was carried out. This means that we shall need to look at six specific issues.

First, we will examine what the research set out to do, and how the aims were clearly formulated. Second, we will examine the various methods available for conducting our research and argue why we settled for using a self completion questionnaire. Third, we will look closely at the way in which the questionnaire was designed and tested out. Fourth, we will look at the geographical area in which the research was located. Fifth, we will discuss the method used for enlisting the co-operation of the churches in the project, and the way in which the churches responded to our approach. Finally, we will discuss the approach made to the teenagers themselves and their response to the questionnaire.

AIMS AND OBJECTIVES

The aims and objectives of the research project were the subject of careful scrutiny by both the working party and the research advisory group. These two groups were concerned both that the results of the research should be of maximum usefulness to the churches and that the method of the research should be of the highest academic standards. They began from the statement of the very general aim of describing the attitudes, values and needs of church-going teenagers. Then they gradually sharpened the objectives into dealing with seven specific questions, or sets of questions, about these young people. These seven sets of questions provide the basis for the rest of this study, so it is worth examining them in some detail.

Who goes to church?

The first group of questions sets out to build up a detailed profile of the teenage church-goers. What proportion of them is male and what proportion is female? How does the pattern of church attendance change between the years of thirteen and twenty? Do some denominations attract more teenagers than others? What proportions of teenage church attenders are still at school, in higher or further education, in work or unemployed? What kind of social background do they come from? Where do they live and what kind of schools have they attended?

Have teenage church-goers generally been brought up within the church? How many of them have been admitted to full membership of their church, and, if so, how were they prepared for this? What kind of services do they tend to go to, and with whom do they tend to go? What is their usual pattern of church attendance? In what kind of church youth groups do they take part? Do they attend weekday bible studies, prayer groups and so on, arranged either specifically for young people or for all ages?

Attitudes to church

The second group of questions sets out to document what the teenagers think about the churches they attend. How do they feel about the kind of services they attend, the older people in the congregation and their ministers? What do they think about the changes that have been made to liturgy and the modern forms of services? How do they feel about the activities arranged by their churches and the priorities these reflect? What changes would they like to see being made? What issues do they feel their churches should be discussing? What kinds of responsibilities do teenagers have or would they like to have in the local church?

Religious belief

The third group of questions was concerned to analyse the religious beliefs and practices of the teenage church attenders. How important is their religion to them? How strong is their belief in God? What do they believe about Jesus, life after death, the resurrection, and so on? What do they believe about the biblical story of creation or about the uniqueness of the Christian revelation? Do they believe in any non-Christian doctrines, like reincarnation, or in any superstitions, like horoscopes?

How devout are these young people in their private religious practices? How often do they read the bible, say prayers, or offer grace before meals? What experience have they had of God influencing their lives? How many of them would claim to have had some form of religious experience, or some form of turning point like a conversion? How much has their experience of religion been confined to just one denomination? How many of them have experienced religious sects or other major world faiths?

Moral and legal attitudes

The fourth group of questions was concerned with a wide range of moral issues. What do teenage church-goers feel about issues related to sexuality, like contraception, pornography, sex outside marriage, homosexuality, divorce and abortion? How do they feel about alcohol, drugs and violence? What are their views on the enforcement of the law over issues like selling cigarettes to children under the legal age, parking restrictions and travelling on public transport without paying for a ticket?

How morally upright do these young people consider themselves? Do they reckon that they ever tell lies, or break their promises? Do they reckon that they are ever guilty of taking advantage of other people, of having feelings of resentment, or of being jealous of others? Have they ever stolen anything? Are they always ready to admit when they have made a mistake?

Political and social attitudes

The fifth group of questions turned attention to the young church-goers' attitudes to the society in which they live. How politically motivated and active are these young people? Which political party do they tend to support? What kind of views do they hold on key matters like unemployment, inflation, nationalisation, immigration and so on? What do they think about trade unions, private medical practice, independent schools? How seriously do they take questions like pollution, nuclear war, the world situation, the poverty of the third world, and so on? Do they feel that their views matter, or do they feel politically helpless?

Work and leisure

The sixth group of questions explored the young church attenders' attitudes to their time at work or school and to their leisure time. How happy are they at school or at work? Are they ambitious in life? Do they get on with the people they work with? Do they often worry about their work? Do they believe in the necessity for hard work, or would they prefer not to work at all if they did not have to do so?

What kind of things do they do in their leisure time? What proportions of them belong to non-church youth groups or sports clubs? How many of them belong to the uniformed organisations, or to regular evening classes or to political groups? How often do they frequent coffee bars, public houses, cinemas, discotheques or bingo halls? How much time do they spend reading, listening to music, listening to the radio or watching television? How many of them are bored with their leisure time?

Well-being and worry

The sixth group of questions looked at the way the young people felt about themselves and about their own lives. How happy are these young people with life? What kinds of things do they worry about? How many of them worry about their physical health, their mental health, their relationships, sex, and so on? How many of them suffer from feelings of loneliness, worthlessness, depression? How many of them have ever felt so fed up with life that their thoughts have turned to suicide?

To whom do these young people turn when they need advice? Do they turn to their parents or to close friends? How many of them ever turn to their ministers for advice or counselling? And if they turn to their ministers for advice, how many of them have been helped by so doing?

CHOICE OF METHOD

After the working party and the research advisory group had agreed on the precise aims and objectives of the research project, the next question concerned the way in which these aims and objectives could best be met. What in fact we required was a great deal of personal information from the teenage church attenders themselves. In the social sciences three main techniques have been advanced for collecting this kind of information: personal interviews, group discussions, and question-naires.

Personal interviews would require a field worker to interview each teenage church-goer individually. This is certainly the best way of getting to know a small number of young people in depth, but it has serious disadvantages when one's main aim is not so much to build up in-depth relationships with a small number of individuals, as to learn something objective about a whole category of people, like teenage church attenders. To begin with, the method is very time-consuming and consequently very expensive. Using this method the project could only have met a limited number of young people. To maximise efficiency, personal interviews need to be conducted in a private and relaxed atmosphere and there was the physical problem of finding the right place in which to interview church-going young people. Often their homes could not provide the right sort of environment. Then there is the problem of the interaction between the interviewer and the young person being interviewed. It is often difficult to know how much the personality of the interviewer is actually influencing the answers given. Finally, there is the problem of recording all that is being said and of making sense of the analysis of the content of the interview.

The group discussion method is obviously cheaper to operate since the interviewer is able to deal with a number of young people at the same time. It is also easier to arrange somewhere, like the church hall, for group discussions to take place. There are, however, a number of reasons why this method would have been unsatisfactory for the present purposes. In the last analysis group discussion among young people tells you a lot more about the pressures and dynamics of the group than about the way in which the individuals in the group actually think and feel. Our project is concerned with individuals, not with groups as such.

When it comes to a consideration of the third method, a clear distinction has to be made between two types of questionnaires, the 'open-ended' and the 'closed-response' formats. The open-ended questionnaire expects the respondents to write out their answers in their own words. This sort of questionnaire would give complete freedom of response to the young people, but again it has a number of serious drawbacks. Taken seriously, an open-ended questionnaire can take a very long time to complete; it can be like writing a number of short essays. Because an open-ended questionnaire depends so much upon the writing skills of the respondent, it can be difficult to judge whether different kinds of answers really reflect differences in basic outlooks, or only differences in written communication skills. This is a particular problem, say, when one is concerned to compare the answers of the non-academic thirteen year old with the nineteen year old undergraduate. Finally, the open-ended questionnaire presents even worse problems in analysis than the personal interview, since there is no method of pushing the respondents to clarify the meaning which they wish to convey by the choice of certain words.

The closed-response questionnaire has been refined by the social sciences as a way of overcoming the problems inherent in the three methods described above. The idea of the closed-response questionnaire is to ask people to select one of a limited range of answers to short and specific questions. This kind of questionnaire is much easier and quicker for the respondent to fill in, and from the researcher's point of view facilitates the analysis of the responses from a large number of people. The two main objections to this method are that it restricts the freedom of some respondents to say all that they might want to say, and that it is open to various kinds of abuse, for example when people answer questions randomly. A great deal of careful work has been conducted by social scientists over the past fifty years to overcome these problems, and largely their efforts have been successful. What is important in the use of a closed-response questionnaire is that a lot of care should be taken in the design and pilot-testing of the instrument before it is set to work collecting the information which will actually be used in the research project.

THE QUESTIONNAIRE

For the reasons outlined above, the present research project is based on a closed-response questionnaire. Two kinds of closed responses are used. Part I of the questionnaire is based on a multiple-choice format. Each question is followed by two or more possible responses and the respondents are asked to tick their preferred choice. For example, against the question 'denomination' all the major Christian denominations are listed so that all the respondent has to do is tick the one to which he or she belongs. Naturally, additional space is provided in the multiple-choice format so that the individual can insert an answer of his or her own if the pre-coded answers should fail to provide a wide enough range of choice.

Part II of the questionnaire is based on what is known as a 'Likert' format. Here the respondents are asked to read a number of short sentences and to assess their level of agreement with these sentences on a five point scale, ranging from 'agree strongly', through 'agree', 'not certain' and 'disagree' to 'disagree strongly'.

The first step in designing a questionnaire of this nature is to listen with care to what young people are themselves saying about the issues with which the study is to be concerned. As far as possible, a good questionnaire should reflect the language used by the people who are to be involved in filling it in.

For the two years preceeding the birth of the present research project, I had been involved in a similar study of the attitudes and values of sixteen to twenty-five year olds. Having spent a long time immersing myself in the culture of this age group, I had already developed and tested a thorough questionnaire, the *Centymca Attitude Inventory*, which covered many of the issues to be explored by the present project. In order to make full use of what had been learnt from my earlier work, the present project incorporated a great deal of the *Centymca Attitude Inventory*.

After talking with a number of young church attenders and after reviewing carefully the usefulness of the *Centymca Attitude Inventory*, a draft questionnaire was put together. This questionnaire was then subjected to three kinds of scrutiny: it was administered to a small group of church-going teenagers, from the age of thirteen to twenty, who volunteered to complete the questionnaire and to talk to me about their reactions to it; it was shown to a number of clergy and parents who were asked how they would feel if such a questionnaire was sent to their own children or to children within their care; and it was thoroughly debated by the working party and the research advisory group.

As a result of these three screening processes, a number of modifications were made to specific items in the questionnaire and one major change was made to the overall shape of the project. There was a group of questions which were thought by several of the clergy to be inappropriate for the younger teenagers. These were mainly moral questions, concerned with issues like human sexuality and drug abuse. The young teenagers themselves who completed the pilot study found neither embarrassment nor difficulty with these issues and indicated that they had firm opinions on them. However, some of the opposition from the clergy was so strong that we felt that the inclusion of such questions for the younger teenagers would lead to some clergy failing to agree to the co-operation of their churches in the whole study. We decided, therefore, that it was politically wise to develop two versions of the questionnaire, a full version for the sixteen to twenty year olds, and a slightly shorter version for the thirteen to fifteen year olds. The only difference between these two editions of the questionnaire is that the shorter version omits the more sensitive questions included in the longer version. In all other respects the information derived from the two versions of the questionnaire is totally compatible.

GEOGRAPHY

Having designed the questionnaire, the next decision concerned the geographical area in which it was to be used. The two limitations placed on the project in making this decision were those of finance and of time. The grants made available to the project could afford to employ a full-time research officer for one year. This meant in effect that we could opt either to make a superficial study over a wide geographical area, or a careful in-depth study over a narrow geographical area.

We decided that the second option would be the more sensible. The research officer would be able to undertake a very thorough job over a limited area. This would mean that the project's contact with the churches could be conducted on a personal level. Personal contact is likely to increase both the co-operation of the churches and the level of response from the young people themselves. It would mean that the research officer could have a firm grasp on the way in which the project was progressing and step in personally to clear up problems and to check potential sources of error. It would also mean that the research officer would be able to learn something about many of the individual churches invited to participate.

The drawback with this option is that we shall not immediately be able to tell how representative our limited geographical area is of England as a whole. However, what can be said is that the findings have rung true for the churches over a much wider area. What we have done, in effect, is to provide both an in-depth study of a limited geographical area and the tools which others can pick up and use in other areas in order to test empirically the extent to which our findings can be generalised.

Since the research officer was based at S. Martin's College, Lancaster, what we decided to do was to select six distinctive geographical areas within Lancashire. The six areas were chosen both for their distinctiveness within the county and in the hope that they would be representative of a particular type of area which could be compared with similar areas in other parts of the country. Richard Basch, the project officer and a trained geographer, visited each of these six areas and described them as follows:

LANCASTER is a cathedral (Roman Catholic) city and a former county town. It has a population of about 50,000. Like much of north Lancashire, Lancaster itself has suffered a considerable degree of unemployment. Its major industries are linoleum, plastic and shoe manufacture.

MORECAMBE includes the resort town and its neighbouring port. It has a population in excess of 40,000. There is some industrial development around both the port and its adjacent nuclear power station.

SKELMERSDALE was designated a new town in 1961 in the south of the county, and built largely to house the overspill from Liverpool. Its current population is about 40,000.

CLITHEROE and the surrounding villages provide an example of a rural area. Clitheroe itself is a market town with about 13,000 inhabitants.

BURNLEY is an old textile town in the eastern half of the county. It has a population of about 92,000.

PRESTON is the county town. Its population of 131,000 makes it the second largest town in Lancashire. Its main industries include textiles, engineering and aircraft manufacture. Because of the size of Preston, only the urban area north of the river Ribble was included in the study. This represents a distinctive unit in its own right.

In order to be objective in our definition of these six areas, the boundaries used were, as far as possible, those of local authorities. In the case of Skelmersdale, the new town development corporation boundary was used. Parish boundaries were used to delimit a defined rural area around Clitheroe.

THE APPROACH TO THE CHURCHES

Having defined the geographical areas in which the research would be undertaken, the next step was to draw up a list of all the churches in those areas. The list included all the Baptist, Churches of Christ, Church of England, Methodist, Roman Catholic, Salvation Army, Society of Friends and United Reformed Church churches.

The aim was then to approach the local leaders of the various denominations, like the Anglican and Roman Catholic bishops, in order to seek their approval for our enquiry and to ask them to commend the project to the clergy with whom we wished to work. We had thought that the fact that the project was initiated by the British Council of Churches, funded by the Department of Education and Science, located in a church college and validated by members of the working party and the research advisory group would commend its seriousness to the church leaders. However, we quickly learnt that the church's work among teenagers was an area in which there was so much fear of failure and guilt, that some of the church leaders refused to sanction the co-operation of their clergy. For example, it proved necessary to exclude the Burnley area from the project completely, because the leader of the denomination which accounted for a sizeable proportion of the total number of churches in the town totally refused to sanction the co-operation of the churches within his care.

In the remaining five areas, the clergy in charge of the churches were asked to help in the project. In total, one hundred and fifty one churches were approached. Again we were surprised by the amount of opposition, both from individual clergy and from whole denominations in some of the areas surveyed. In three of the five areas a whole denomination withdrew en bloc, but since these denominations were content to co-operate in other areas we decided that, while this was unfortunate, it would not ultimately prove detrimental to the whole study.

All told, 28% of the churches approached actually refused to take part in the survey or used delaying tactics which made their church's participation in the survey impossible. For example, one minister approached in October would not proceed with the project until he had obtained the approval of one church committee in December and the confirmation of the church council the following February. Underlying many of the specific objections raised by the clergy was a mistrust and anxiety that their relationships with their congregation and those on the fringe of their churches would be damaged by their participation in the project. Some were also concerned about the questions on sex and drugs, about the danger that the questionnaire would put doubts and anxieties into the minds of young people, and about the way in which the questionnaire invited young people to evaluate their own churches.

A further 13% of the churches, while not refusing to take part in the survey, proved so elusive that they had to be excluded. For example, there were those churches where the clergy never answered letters and never seemed to be at home to answer the telephone. There were also some that agreed to take part in the survey, and then on the appointed day failed to organise their participation in an effective manner.

Thus, of the one hundred and fifty one churches approached, ninety actually took part in the project, representing a 59% response. More detailed breakdown of the churches included in the survey is provided in Table 2.1. Given all the difficulties encountered, such a high response is due largely to the project officer's persistence and tact.

THE APPROACH TO THE TEENAGERS

The ninety churches co-operating in the project were all asked to proceed in the same fashion. The clergyman in charge of the church nominated a lay person to be responsible for the project. The project officer then visited these lay people and talked through the design of the study with them. In this way there was one person in every church who really understood what the project was all about and who generally felt highly committed to promoting its success.

The aim was to appoint a specific Sunday for each of the five geographical areas so that every participating church in the area made its contribution on the same Sunday. In this way we were able to spread the five areas over different parts of the year to enable the project officer to concentrate on one area at a time.

On the appointed Sunday, the clergyman was asked to mention the project briefly at every service in the church and to ask the teenagers to co-operate. The job of the lay person responsible for the project was to make sure that there was a team of leaders ready to talk to all the teenagers attending church on that Sunday and to ask all of them between the ages of thirteen and twenty inclusive to complete a small index card giving their name and address.

All told, 1902 young people completed a registration card on the nominated Sunday. This means that there was an average of twenty one teenagers in touch with each of the ninety churches on a typical Sunday. The average, however, conceals a great deal of variation among individual churches. For example, seven of the participating churches reported no contact with any teenagers on the nominated Sunday, while another church reported contact with one hundred and seventy two teenagers. While on average forty six teenagers had contact with each of the twenty two participating Roman Catholic churches, only an average of three teenagers had contact with each of the two Salvation Army citadels or the three Society of Friends meeting houses (see Table 2.2).

When the completed registration cards had been returned to the project officer, he posted a copy of the questionnaire to the young people. A reminder letter, together with a further copy of the questionnaire, was sent to all those who had not completed and returned their questionnaire approximately one month after the original mailing. In total, 1328 of the 1902 teenagers returned their questionnaire completely and thoroughly answered, and suitable for analysis. Part-completed questionnaires were not regarded as suitable for inclusion in the analysis and so they were treated as the equivalent of a failure to respond at all. This means that there were satisfactory responses from 70% of the sample.

The 70% response rate is very high in terms of what can usually be expected from postal surveys. This helps to indicate how motivated the teenage church attenders were to participate in a project of this nature. It also indicates how the young people were much more willing to co-operate in this kind of study than were some of their churches and clergy.

Not only did a high proportion of the young people respond to the survey, but the majority of those who did respond said that they had enjoyed doing so. Although the questionnaire required a great deal of thought, care and time, less than 8% said that they had failed to enjoy the exercise. The boys were more likely than the girls to place themselves in this small minority, as were the Anglicans rather than the Roman Catholics or the members of the Free Churches.

3 TEENAGE CHURCH-GOERS

Before looking at the attitudes of the teenage church attenders in the following chapters, it is sensible to begin by saying as much as we can about who these young people are who filled in the detailed attitude inventory. With this aim in mind, the present chapter sets out to do two things.

First, we want to know as much as possible about their background and who they are. What churches do they represent? What is the ratio between the boys and girls among the teenage church-goers? How many thirteen year olds are there in church for every twenty year old church-goer? What kind of schools have these young people attended? How many of them are still at school, and what are those who have left school now doing? What is their social background, and so on?

Second, we want to know what kind of involvement these young people actually have with their church. How many of them attend service every Sunday, and how many of them are more casual attenders? What kind of services do they attend? With whom do they go to church? Do they look to their families for support, or do they prefer to go with friends of their own age? At what age are these young people admitted to full membership of their church, and what kind of preparation do they receive before admission? What kind of church activities do they support, apart from Sunday services?

SOCIOLOGICAL DESCRIPTION

Denomination

When the study was set up, it was hoped that all the churches of the main denominations located within the specified geographical areas would co-operate with the study. Had all the denominations co-operated to the same extent, one of the important things we could have learnt from the project would have been the relative strength of the denominations in these areas, in terms of the number of teenagers they attracted. However, since the willingness of the churches to participate varied from 70% of the Anglican churches approached to only 31% of the Methodist churches, any such comparison is made much more speculative.

The number of teenagers from each denomination responding to the survey is obviously related to the number of churches from each denomination co-operating in the project. Just 26 of the 1328 young people who returned their questionnaire did not divulge their denomination. Of those who did identify their denomination, 640 (49%) were Roman Catholics, 455 (35%) were Church of England, 83 (6%) were Methodists, 45 (3%) were members of the United Reformed Church or the Churches of Christ, 43 (3%) were Baptists, 10 (1%) belonged to the Society of Friends and 3 belonged to the Salvation Army. There were also 3 Pentecostal, 2 Brethren, 1 Church of Scotland, and 1 member of an Independent Free Evangelical Church. 4 of the young people called themselves ecumenical and one preferred the title 'non-conformist'. The remaining 11 said that they owned allegiance to no particular denomination. Thus, it seemed that a very small minority of the young people attending the church services included in the survey were regarding themselves as visitors to these churches, while retaining allegiance to some other denomination. The vast majority, however, were clearly worshipping in churches of the denomination to which they felt they belonged.

For the purposes of the rest of this study, the teenagers who belonged to the Baptist, Churches of Christ, Methodist, Salvation Army, and United Reformed Church groups will be classified together and described as members of the Free Churches. Unfortunately, the numbers responding from the respective denominations which constitute the Free Church group were not sufficient to allow these denominations to be analysed separately. The main comparisons reported in the rest of this book are, therefore, based on 640 Roman Catholics, 455 Anglicans and 175 members of the Free Churches.

Sex

It is a well documented sociological fact that women show a greater interest in religion than men. There is certainly no exception to this rule among teenage church attenders. 789 (59%) of the 1328 teenagers in the sample were female. This means that, overall, there are roughly 6 teenage girls going to church for every 4 teenage boys.

This ratio between the sexes remained basically constant both across the teenage age range and between the various churches. Thus, 59% of the younger teenagers (thirteen to fifteen year olds) and 60% of the older teenagers (sixteen to twenty year olds) were female. Similarly 61% of the Anglicans, 60% of the members of the Free Churches and 57% of the Roman Catholics were female.

Age

Interest in church quickly and consistently declines during the teenage years. Roughly speaking, for every 24 thirteen or fourteen year old church-goers we can expect there to be 22 fifteen year olds, 19 sixteen year olds, 15 seventeen year olds, 11 eighteen year olds, 8 nineteen year olds and 7 twenty year olds. In other words, it looks as if 71% of the teenagers who go to church at the age of fourteen would have stopped doing so by the time they reach the age of twenty.

The likelihood of young teenage church attenders drifting away from the church during the later teenage years is much higher in the Church of England than in either the Roman Catholic or the Free Churches. The best way of illustrating this point is to compare the number of eighteen to twenty year olds with the number of thirteen to fifteen year olds in the different churches. In the Church of England there is drop of 74% between these two age groups, compared with 55% in the Roman Catholic Church and 49% in the Free Churches. In other words, it looks as if half of the young people who attend Roman Catholic or Free Churches and three quarters of those who attend Church of England churches between the ages of thirteen and fifteen would have stopped going to church by the ages of eighteen to twenty.

School

8% of the teenage church-goers have received all or most of their secondary education in an independent school, while the other 92% have been educated within the state maintained sector. Within the state maintained sector of secondary schools, there are those wholly supported by the state and those originally founded by voluntary bodies like the churches. In Lancashire, 70% of the children in state maintained secondary schools are in schools provided wholly by the local education authority, while 22% are in Roman Catholic voluntary maintained schools and 8% are in Church of England voluntary maintained schools.

First, we will examine the extent to which attendance at a denominational school is associated with teenage church attendance. To begin with, a much higher proportion of teenage church-goers have attended a church voluntary school than the proportion of the population at large. While Roman Catholic schools account for just 22% of the state provided secondary school places in Lancashire they account for 50% of the teenage church attenders not educated in independent schools. While Church of England schools account for just 8% of the state provided secondary school places in Lancashire, they account for 14% of the teenage church attenders not educated in independent schools. In order to complete the picture, the county schools provide 70% of the places and account for the remaining 36% of teenage church attenders.

Second, we will examine the relationship between the type of school attended and the denomination of the church attended. The vast majority (92%) of the teenagers attending Roman Catholic churches have been educated in the Roman Catholic voluntary school system. Just over 4% of them have attended a county secondary school, and less than 1% have attended a Church of England voluntary secondary school. The remaining 3% have been educated in the independent sector.

Just one in three (31%) of the teenagers attending Church of England churches have been educated in a Church of England voluntary secondary school. 55% of them have attended a county secondary school, and just 1% have attended a Roman Catholic voluntary secondary school. The remaining 13% have been educated in the independent sector.

In the case of the Free Churches, three quarters (74%) of the teenage church-goers have attended county secondary schools. 11% of them have attended Church of England voluntary secondary schools, and just 1% have attended Roman Catholic voluntary secondary schools. The remaining 14% have been educated in the independent sector.

Third, we will examine the extent to which the influence of the type of secondary school attended extends into the later teenage years. Exactly the same proportions of the younger teenage and the older teenage church attenders were educated in county schools or independent schools. The differences come when we compare those educated in Roman Catholic and in Church of England state maintained secondary schools. Only 9% of the sixteen to twenty year old church attenders were educated in a Church of England secondary school, compared with 16% of the thirteen to fifteen year olds. On the other hand, 50% of the sixteen to twenty year old church attenders were educated in a Roman Catholic secondary school, compared with 43% of the thirteen to fifteen year olds.

This means that those educated in Roman Catholic state maintained secondary schools are less likely to drift away from the church as they grow older than those educated in county schools. It also means that those educated in Church of England state maintained secondary schools are more likely to drift away from the church as they grow older than those educated in county schools. Not only has the Roman Catholic Church a much stronger stake in state maintained secondary education than the Church of England, but it would also seem that those educated in Roman Catholic schools are likely to have a more lasting relationship with the church than those educated in Church of England schools. This difference is likely to be the consequence of a complex set of relationships between school, home and church.

Social class

Social class, or socio-economic status, is often determined in social research on the basis of the social grading, or prestige, of different forms of employment. There are several occupational classification systems currently in use, but the most frequently used scale is the five point categorisation prepared by the Government Office of Population, Censuses and Surveys. It is this system that is currently used in the analysis of many official statistics. This scale is a classification of occupations (or to be more precise 'unit groups' of occupations) according to 'the general standing within the community of the occupations concerned'.

According to this classification system, professionals, like doctors or accountants, solicitors and clergymen, are assigned to social class one. Semi-professionals, like teachers, social workers, journalists and entertainers are assigned to social class two. Social class three includes skilled occupations, like bus drivers, clerks, secretaries and electricians. Social class four includes postmen, machine operators, bricklayers and bus conductors. Social class five includes the unskilled manual labourers, porters and messengers.

Each of the teenagers who completed the attitude inventory were asked to provide a description of both their mother's and their father's occupation. On the basis of this information we were able to assign their parents to one of the five social categorisations. And on this basis we are able to say something about the social background of the teenagers who go to church.

The teenage church-goers tend to come from the higher social class backgrounds. Thus, while only 4% of men employed in Lancashire are in social class one occupations, 14% of the teenage church-goers come from this kind of professional background. Similarly, while only 17% of men employed in Lancashire are in social class two occupations, 29% of the teenage church-goers come from this kind of semi-professional background. At the other end of the scale, while 27% of the men employed in Lancashire have social class four or five occupations, only 10% of the teenage church-goers come from the semi-skilled or unskilled backgrounds.

The next thing to note is that there are some interesting differences in the socio-economic backgrounds of teenagers associated with different denominations. The Free Churches have the largest proportion of young people from the higher social classes, while the Roman Catholic churches have the smallest proportion of young people from the higher social classes. Thus, 21% of the Free Church members, 17% of the Anglicans and only 10% of the Roman Catholic teenagers come from professional backgrounds. 32% of the Free Church teenagers, 31% of the Anglicans and 25% of the Roman Catholics come from semi-professional backgrounds. At the other end of the scale, 5% of the Free Church teenagers and 8% of the Anglican teenagers are from semi-skilled or unskilled backgrounds, compared with 12% of the Roman Catholic teenagers.

A similar set of differences emerges between the denominations when the mother's occupational status is used to determine the social class of the teenagers. Once again, the Roman Catholic group has the lowest proportion (33%) employed in social class one or two occupations, compared with 37% of the Anglicans and 38% of the Free Church members. Similarly, the Roman Catholic group has the highest proportion (23%) employed in social class four or five occupations, compared with 16% of the Free Church members and 15% of the Anglicans.

Occupation

Three fifths (58%) of the sixteen to twenty year old church attenders are still engaged in some form of full-time education. 22% of them were still at school, while 36% of them were studying at an institute of further or higher education, a technical college, a college of education, a university and so on. A further 10% of them, having left full-time education to begin to earn a living, were at the same time still involved in some form of part-time education, like day-release schemes. 26% of the sixteen to twenty year old church-goers were in full-time employment, without simultaneously undertaking further education. The remaining 6% of these young people were unemployed.

The older teenage church attenders emerge as an intelligent and academically successful group. 52% of the young church attenders aged sixteen or over have obtained five or more O levels, and a number of them have either already obtained A levels or are on their way to obtaining them.

The 36% of the sixteen to twenty year old church-goers who are in work have undertaken a wide and interesting range of jobs. Among the young men in the sample there is a fishmonger, a butcher and a butcher's apprentice; a trainee chef and a waiter; a general agricultural worker, a gardener and a trainee farm manager; a salesman from a photographic and electrical firm, a sales representative for a clothing firm, and a trainee shop manager; a postman and a telephone wireman; a labourer for a construction company and a furniture remover; a carpenter making kitchen units, an apprentice welder, a maintenance fitter, an apprentice engineer and a tool maker; a weaver in a bandage factory, a carpet fitter and a photo-type setter; a houseparent in a community home and a laboratory technician in the printing ink manufacturing industry; a clerical assistant in the civil service, a bank clerk and a buiding society cashier; and several trainees on work experience programmes created for the young unemployed.

Among the young women who are in work, there is a sewing machinist, a junior machine operator and an assembler working on circuit boards; a policewoman and a forensic science laboratory technician; a production worker in a factory making toiletries and a ledger clerk for a security firm; a hairdresser and a Swedish au pair; a telephonist, a wages clerk, a VDU operator, a secretary and a receptionist; a solicitor's clerk, a trainee accountant and a civil servant in the Department of Health and Social Security; a sales assistant in a dress shop, a cashier in a supermarket and a stock controller in a chemist; a pupil nurse, a student nurse and a nursing auxiliary; a clerical assistant, an audio copy typist, a shorthand typist, a clerk and an invoice typist; a personal secretary in a social work department of a psychiatric unit and an assistant nursery nurse in a school for mentally and physically handicapped children; a bank clerk and an assistant in the planning office of a hosiery factory; and several trainees on work experience programmes for the young unemployed.

Marital status

The majority (90%) of the young people who continue to attend church after the school leaving age still live at home with their parents. Many of the other 10% of the sample are accounted for by the students attending the university or colleges within the catchment areas selected for the study.

Only a small minority of the older church-going teenagers have formed stable relationships outside their parental home. 8% of the sixteen to twenty year old girls are engaged, and a further 1% are married. None of the sixteen to twenty year old youths are married, and only 2% are engaged. Just one of the young men in the sample says that he is living with his girlfriend.

CHURCH INVOLVEMENT

Church attendance

In order to be included in the study in the first place, all the young people had attended at least one church service on the Sunday on which the sample was constituted. How many of these young people try to attend a service every Sunday, and how many of them are casual attenders who just happened to be around on the Sunday chosen for our survey? In other words, what level of commitment can we expect to find among the teenagers who appear in church congregations on any given Sunday?

Nearly two thirds of the teenage church-goers (65%) claim to be committed to weekly attendance and to have attended services on all the four previous consecutive Sundays. A further 16% said that they have missed only one Sunday during the past four weeks. In other words, only one in five of the young people in church on a given Sunday are likely to be casual church-goers. This statistic has two important implications for the churches. It means that they can presuppose a high level of commitment among the majority of their young attenders, but it also means that at any given time they are making comparatively little contact with the young people who are on the fringe of church commitment.

There are no significant sex differences in the regularity of Sunday church attendance, but there are some significant age differences and differences between the various denominations. The older teenagers who attend church are more likely to be committed to attending every Sunday. While 62% of the thirteen to fifteen year olds say that they have attended church every Sunday within the past month, the proportion rises to 70% of the sixteen to twenty year olds. By the time they have reached this older age group, there is a greater tendency for the young people who are not committed to weekly church attendance to have stopped going to church altogether.

It has already been shown in an earlier section of this chapter that the Church of England is less successful in keeping its young church attenders into their late teens than either the Roman Catholic Church or the Free Churches. In a similar way, teenagers who attend Church of England services are less likely to be weekly church-goers than those who attend Roman Catholic or Free Church services. Thus, only 52% of the older teenagers in the sample who claim allegiance to the Church of England say that they have attended services every Sunday during the past four weeks, compared with 67% of their contemporaries who attend the Free Churches and 81% of the Roman Catholics.

The vast majority of teenage church attenders (84%) will attend just one service on a Sunday. Overall this proportion remains roughly constant throughout the age range and for both sexes. There is, however, quite a variation between the denominations and this variation becomes more pronounced among the older teenagers. The Roman Catholics are least likely to attend more than one service on a Sunday. Only 8% of the thirteen to fifteen year old Roman Catholics and 4% of the sixteen to twenty year olds attended more than one service on the previous Sunday. On the other hand, the members of the Free Churches are much more likely to attend church twice on a Sunday and this likelihood increases with age. 25% of the thirteen to fifteen year old Free Church members and 40% of the sixteen to twenty year olds attended more than one service on the previous Sunday. The Church of England occupies a midway position, with 19% of the thirteen to fifteen year old members and 26% of the sixteen to twenty year olds attending more than one Sunday service.

The most popular times for teenagers to attend church are those services which begin between 9.00 a.m. and 11.00 a.m. on a Sunday. This is true for both sexes and for all three denominational groups throughout the whole age range. By way of comparison, the teenagers show little interest in attending early morning, late morning or afternoon services. The second most popular time for going to church is in the evening. This is particularly the case among the older teenage members of the Free Churches, who are likely to be attending their second service of the day at around 6.30 p.m. Among the sixteen to twenty year olds, 26% of the Roman Catholics, 26% of the Anglicans and 48% of the Free Church members who attended church the previous Sunday chose to go to an evening service.

The importance of attending communion on a Sunday is very clearly related to denominational background. 99% of the Roman Catholics throughout the age range who attend a Sunday service are present at a celebration of the mass. Communion is both less central in the Free Churches and also something less likely to be attended by children and young people. Thus, 45% of the Free Church teenagers aged between thirteen and fifteen and 56% of those aged between sixteen and twenty who attend a Sunday service are present at a communion service. In the case of the Church of England, communion is given a more central place than in the Free Churches and a less central place than in the Roman Catholic Church. Thus, 74% of the Church of England young people aged between thirteen and fifteen and 79% of those aged between sixteen and twenty who attend a Sunday service are present at a celebration of communion.

Two thirds (66%) of the teenagers who go to church on a Sunday are unlikely generally to consider attending weekday services as well. On the other hand, 9% tend to go to at least one weekday service every week, while the other 25% tend to go to a weekday service at least once a month. It is the thirteen to fifteen year old Roman Catholics who are most likely to attend a weekday service at least monthly (48%) and the Anglicans of the same age who are least likely so to do (26%).

Family support

The teenagers who go to church on a Sunday generally tend to go in the company of other people. Although the proportion of teenagers who attend church alone increases with age, still less than a quarter of the sixteen to twenty year olds say that this is the case for them. It is the young people who go to the Free Churches who are least likely to go alone and those who go to the Roman Catholic churches who are most likely to go alone. Among the thirteen to fifteen year olds, 3% of the Free Church members, 14% of the Anglicans and 13% of the Roman Catholics go to services alone, while among the sixteen to twenty year olds, the proportions increase to 11% of the Free Church members, 23% of the Anglicans and 28% of the Roman Catholics.

It is the family rather than friends which gives the greater support to teenage church-goers and, within the family, it is the mother who plays the major role. All told, more than half (52%) of the teenagers who go to church go with their mother. The mother has an influence on larger proportions of the thirteen to fifteen year olds (57%) than the sixteen to twenty year olds (46%), the boys (57%) than the girls (48%), the Free

Church members (65%) and the Roman Catholics (57%) than the Anglicans (41%).

These interesting differences according to age, sex and denomination are also clearly reflected by the proportions of young people who say that they go to church with their father or with brothers or sisters. Overall, the support of brothers and sisters is important to 42% of church-going teenagers, while the support of their father is important to 35%. Looked at by denominations separately, 53% of the Free Church members, 39% of the Roman Catholics and 25% of the Anglicans go to church with their father, while 50% of the Free Church members, 47% of the Roman Catholics and 32% of the Anglicans go to church with their brothers or sisters.

Although overall grandparents do not play an important part in teenage church attendance, the small part which they play follows closely the same denominational pattern, with the greatest family support being given in the Free Churches and the least in the Church of England. Thus, among the thirteen to fifteen year olds, 12% of those who worship in the Free Churches, 8% in the Roman Catholic Church and 3% in the Church of England attend with their grandparents.

Just a quarter (25%) of teenage church attenders go to church with friends of their own age. However, it is important to note that the support of friends is strongest where the support of families is weakest. Thus, girls (30%) are more likely to go to church with friends of their own age than boys (19%), and Anglicans are more likely to do so than either the young members of the Free Churches or the Roman Catholic Church. The denominational differences are seen most clearly among the thirteen to fifteen year olds, when 40% of the Anglican teenagers go to church with friends of their own age, compared with 19% of the Free Church teenagers and 11% of the Roman Catholics.

These statistics reflect an important difference in the way in which the denominations recruit young church attenders. The Free Churches and the Roman Catholic Church seem to recruit much more exclusively from within the families of their practising membership. The Anglican Church seems to recruit on a wider basis. This observation needs to be read in association with the statistics quoted earlier regarding the lapse rate during the teenage years. The denomination which recruits young teenagers most successfully from among those who have no parental support also loses its young members most quickly as they grow into the later teens. The family seems to remain of major importance in fostering teenage church membership.

Adult membership

The ages at which young people are admitted into adult membership of their churches differ significantly from denomination to denomination. What this means in practice with the teenage church-goers in the sample can be seen most clearly if we restrict our examination to the sixteen to twenty year olds.

Only a small fraction (1%) of the sixteen to twenty year olds who attend the Roman Catholic Church have not been received into adult membership through confirmation. Indeed, the majority of them had been confirmed before they left primary school. 35% had been confirmed before their tenth birthday and a further 35% had been confirmed when they were ten or eleven.

Just one in ten (10%) of the sixteen to twenty year olds who attend the Church of England have not been received into adult membership through confirmation. Confirmation in the Church of England generally takes place later than in the Roman Catholic Church, although the Church of England is far from being of one mind as to the best age for confirmation to happen. In practice, the bulk of Anglican confirmations seems to take place between the eleventh and fifteenth birthdays. Only 5% of the young Anglicans were confirmed before the age of eleven. 19% were confirmed at the age of eleven, 21% at twelve, 14% at thirteen, 19% at fourteen and just 7% at fifteen. This means that only a very small proportion of church-going Anglican teenagers are confirmed after the age of fifteen.

In the case of the Free Churches, admission to adult membership tends to be left to the mid-adolescent years. Thus, over a quarter (27%) of the sixteen to twenty year olds who attend the Free Churches have not been admitted into adult membership. Just 14% of them were admitted to adult membership before their fourteenth birthday; 9% were admitted at the age of fourteen, 12% at fifteen and 25% at sixteen. This means that young people are still being steadily admitted to full membership of the Free Churches during their late teens.

Before being admitted into full membership of their respective denominations, the majority of the sixteen to twenty year olds (85%) had undertaken a special period of instruction, for example confirmation classes. The weight which the different denominations give to special preparation at this stage depends on a number of factors: for example, the importance they attach to the actual admission to membership, the extent to which they regard regular church attendance over the previous years as the most important form of preparation, and the actual resources which the local churches can muster for running special training programmes.

The Church of England seems to give the most importance to running something like confirmation classes. This may well be related to the two facts that the Church of England tends to recruit teenage members whose parents are not active church-goers and that the Church of England often provides no other type of formal instruction for its young people. Thus, only 13% of the Anglican teenagers were admitted to adult membership with less than a month's special preparation, compared with 27% of the Free Church members and 39% of the Roman Catholics.

When special classes are run, the favoured duration is between one and six months. 35% of the Roman Catholics, 35% of the Anglicans and 49% of the Free Church members experienced a provision of between one and three months, while 14% of the Roman Catholics, 34% of the Anglicans and 17% of the Free Church members experienced a provision of between four and six months. This means that just 12% of the Roman Catholics, 17% of the Anglicans and 7% of the Free Church teenagers experienced more than six months special preparation before being admitted into adult membership.

Church activities

Apart from going to services on a Sunday, and sometimes during the week as well, in what other ways do the teenage church-goers become involved in the life of their local church? To begin with we will examine how much they are involved in activities provided by the church specifically for young people, then we will broaden the question and examine how much they are involved in all age activities provided by their churches.

Of the range of church activities in which teenagers participate, church youth clubs seem to have the most important part to play in the lives of teenage church members. 40% of the thirteen to fifteen year olds and 29% of the sixteen to twenty year olds had attended a church youth club within the past three months. The next most important provision concerns church sponsored uniformed organisations, like the scouts and guides. 16% of the thirteen to fifteen year olds and 6% of the sixteen to twenty year olds had attended a church sponsored company of guides or scouts within the past three months.

On the other hand, there is much less experience on the part of teenage church-goers of belonging to more explicitly religious groups for young people. Young people's bible study groups are supported by 3% of the thirteen to fifteen year olds and 7% of the sixteen to twenty year olds. The denominational differences here are most clearly seen among the older group: 22% of the Free Church sixteen to twenty year olds have been to a young persons' bible study group within the past three months, compared with 7% of the Anglicans and 1% of the Roman Catholics.

Young people's prayer groups are supported by 3% of the thirteen to fifteen year olds and 8% of the sixteen to twenty year olds. Here the denominational differences are getting less marked: 18% of the Free Church sixteen to twenty year olds have been to a young persons' prayer group within the last three months, compared with 6% of the Anglicans and 6% of the Roman Catholics.

Within the past three months, less than 2% of teenage church-goers have had experience of being involved in a young persons' house communion group, a young persons' evangelistic group or a young persons' community service group. Within the past three months, just 4% have been involved in a young persons' informal house group, 4% have been involved in a young persons' study group, and 7% have been involved in a young persons' music group run by the church.

The overall picture, therefore, suggests that very few teenage church-goers are being nurtured in the Christian faith through provisions which their churches are arranging specifically for young people. The picture is no more promising when we turn attention to the number of church-going teenagers involved in provisions made by their churches for the adult members.

Within the past three months, of the sixteen to twenty year old church attenders, just 7% have attended an adult bible study group, 7% a prayer group, 6% an informal house group, 4% a study group, 2% a house communion group, 2% an overseas mission project, 1% an evangelistic group, and 1% a community service group. Among the sixteen to twenty year olds, it is the members of the Free Churches who are most likely to be involved in adult groups of one sort or another and the young Roman Catholics who are least likely to be so involved. For example, 20% of the Free Church members have attended an all-age bible group within the past three months, compared with 9% of the Anglicans and 1% of the Roman Catholics. 17% of the Free Church members have attended an all-age prayer group, compared with 5% of the Anglicans and 5% of the Roman Catholics. 12% of the Free Church members have attended an all-age study group, compared with 4% of the Anglicans and 1% of the Roman Catholics.

The kind of all-age group best supported by the Anglicans is the informal house meeting: informal house meetings arranged for adults as well as for teenagers have attracted just 10% of the sixteen to twenty year old Anglicans within the past three months. The kind of all-age group best supported by the Roman Catholics is the prayer group: prayer groups arranged for teenagers as well as for adults have attracted just 5% of the sixteen to twenty year old Roman Catholics within the past three months.

By way of summary, these statistics make it clear that for the majority of teenage church-goers their involvement with the churches is limited mainly to Sundays and then mainly to attending services.

4 CHURCH MEMBERSHIP

Our review of the attitudes of the teenage church attenders in the sample begins by examining what it means to them to belong to a local church. This analysis is divided into four distinct areas.

The first section reviews the *activities* which teenagers undertake in the church. How much opportunity are they given to perform some active role in worship, and what kinds of activities are they given to do? To what extent do teenagers wish to take a more active role in worship than in fact they have the opportunity to take at present?

The second section reviews the *responsibilities* which teenagers hold in order to further the life and work of their local church. What kind of responsibilities are most generally given to teenage church-goers, and how willing would they be to accept a different or wider range of responsibilities?

The third section examines the *topics* which teenagers have the opportunity to discuss when they attend church groups. What topics are most frequently on the agenda of their local groups? How happy are they with this agenda, and are there other topics which they feel should be more generally or openly discussed?

The fourth section turns attention to the *priorities* which the teenagers feel should count in their local church. If teenage church-goers were able to influence the programme of their local church, would they want to see more weight given to a social gospel, a spirtual gospel, a political gospel, or what?

ACTIVITIES

When teenagers go to church, how much opportunity are they given to perform some active role in the service and what kinds of activities are they given to do?

The activity most entrusted to young people is that of taking the collection. One in three (33%) of the teenagers who attend church, irrespective of where they come within the age band under review, are invited to do this at least occasionally. Their chances of being invited to take the collection are slightly higher if they are male (36%) than if they are female (31%). Their chances are much higher if they attend one of the Free churches (67%) than if they attend the Church of England (34%) or the Roman Catholic Church (23%).

Next in line, after taking the collection, are helping to make the coffee after the service, reading lessons, giving out the books and singing in the choir. While taking the collection is regarded as a more appropriate task for the boys than for the girls, making the coffee is regarded overwhelmingly as a female task. 30% of the girls who attend church are sometimes invited to do this, compared with 13% of the boys. Again, the young members of the Free Churches are much more likely to be involved in this way (56%) than those who attend the Church of England (25%) or the Roman Catholic Church (11%).

27% of the teenagers who attend church are sometimes invited to read lessons. Their chances of reading lessons are higher if they are aged sixteen or over (31%) than if they are under sixteen (23%), if they are female (29%) rather than male (24%), and if they attend one of the Free Churches (51%) rather than an Anglican church (30%) or a Roman Catholic church (18%).

One in four (25%) of the teenagers are invited to give out the books in church at least occasionally. This time, the girls and the boys stand equal chances, but once again their chances are higher in the Free Churches (41%) than in the Church of England (30%) or the Roman Catholic Church (17%). Although giving out the books before the service can be an important way of making contact with people and of welcoming visitors to the service, many of the young people who are given this task understand it purely in the functional terms of seeing that the congregation have the right books to use. While 33% of the young people are employed to give out books, only 16% feel that their job really involves the responsibility of welcoming visitors into their church.

24% of the teenagers who go to church sometimes contribute to the church choir, and as many as 13% of them do so weekly. Church choirs contain many more younger teenagers than older teenagers, but their withdrawal from the church choir as the teenagers grow older is no more marked than their withdrawal from church itself. Thus, roughly the same proportions of thirteen to fifteen year old and sixteen to twenty year old church-going teenagers take an interest in the choir.

The girls who go to church are more likely to show an interest in the choir (28%) than the boys (18%). There are no great denominational differences on this issue: choirs attract 28% of the Anglican church-goers, 26% of the Free Church attenders and 23% of those who attend Roman Catholic churches.

Another way in which young musicians are involved in worship is through inviting them to play musical instruments. 12% of the teenagers have had this experience, 7% of the boys and 15% of the girls. It is the Free Churches with their smaller membership which give the most opportunity to teenage musicians (23%), compared with 12% of the Anglicans and 9% of the Roman Catholics.

While choristers and instrumentalists tend to be female, altar serving and bell ringing have remained largely male-dominated activities. 28% of the young male church attenders, compared with only 4% of the girls, have had some experience of altar serving. 8% of the young male church attenders, compared with only 3% of the girls, have had some experience of bell ringing.

Activities like taking the collection, making the coffee, giving out books, and even singing in the choir, are all functions which give very little room for initiative and do little to develop leadership skills. It is the exception rather than the rule for even the sixteen to twenty year olds to be given the occasional opportunity to exercise real leadership in worship, unless they belong to one of the Free Churches. The proportion of young people in this age group who feel that they have been invited to help in actually conducting worship amounts to one in three hundred among the Roman Catholics, one in twenty-five among the Anglicans and one in five among the Free Church members.

Turning to the leadership of specific aspects of worship, 1% of the Roman Catholics, 2% of the Anglicans and 7% of the Free Church members have had the experience of preaching. 6% of the Roman Catholics, 17% of the Anglicans and 23% of the Free Church members have led the prayers in worship. 3% of the Roman Catholics, 15% of the Anglicans and 18% of the Free Church members have been involved in drama in worship. 3% of the Roman Catholics, 4% of the Anglicans and 2% of the Free Church members have taken part in liturgical dance.

Having reviewed the extent to which young people are already actively involved in worship, we need to turn attention to those who are not actively involved and discover whether this is a matter of choice or of circumstance. Generally speaking, the young church-goers do not appear to be clamouring for much more involvement than has already been granted to them, and their sights seem to be set on doing those jobs which other teenagers already most frequently undertake. Somewhere between one in five and one in seven of the church-going teenagers have an unfulfilled ambition to welcome visitors (20%), ring the bells (20%), make the coffee after the service (19%), take the collection (16%) or give out the books (15%).

More significantly, there seems to be quite a lot of untapped talent which would like to find fulfilment preparing drama for church services (16%) and in providing instrumental music to accompany worship (15%). 12% would like to read lessons and are never given the opportunity; 10% would like to serve and never have the opportunity to do so; 9% think they would like to be part of the choir but have never joined; 6% feel that they would like the opportunity to undertake liturgical dance, and these are mainly Anglican girls.

When it comes to the major leadership functions in worship, like helping in conducting worship, leading prayers and preaching, even the sixteen to twenty year olds do not generally feel that this is something they wish to undertake. It is the Roman Catholic young people who are both least accustomed to helping in conducting worship and also least anxious to assume such a function. The structure of their church does not encourage them to think in this kind of way. Thus only 0.3% of the Roman Catholic sixteen to twenty year olds report that they have had the experience of helping to conduct worship and only 4% wish that they had been given such an opportunity. By way of comparison, the Free Churches have already encouraged 20% of their older teenagers to feel that they have given help in conducting worship and left untapped a further 8% who want the experience but have been unable to find an opportunity for it. The Anglican Church has given the opportunity to just 4% of its older teenagers and left untapped a further 12% who want the experience but have been unable to find an opportunity for it.

Similarly, among the sixteen to twenty year olds, 19% of the Anglicans, 13% of the Free Church members and just 6% of the Roman Catholics say that they have not had the opportunity to lead prayers and would like to do so. 12% of the Anglicans, 11% of the Free Church members and just 2% of the Roman Catholics say that they have not had the opportunity to preach and would like to do so.

RESPONSIBILITIES

Churches tend to function like many other voluntary associational activities which are able to afford to employ only a very small full-time executive in relationship both to the number of members and the range and scope of the activities which the membership wishes its association to undertake. In theory, this means that there is an almost inexhaustible range of responsibilities which the membership needs to undertake in a voluntary capacity if the church is to fulfil its function. To what extent are teenage church-goers encouraged to take up such responsibilities?

The responsibility most frequently accepted by teenagers in the Church of England and the Free Churches is that of teaching in the Sunday school. Already by the time they have reached the age of fifteen, 9% of the teenagers who attend either the Church of England or one of the Free Churches have been enlisted as Sunday school teachers. Among the sixteen to twenty year olds, this proportion increases to 20% of the Anglicans and 31% of the Free Church members. Moreover, Sunday school teaching is still seen very much as a female activity. The teenage girls who attend church are four times as likely to become Sunday school teachers as the teenage boys. Given the fact that many more girls attend church anyway, this means that there are eleven teenage girls teaching in Sunday schools for every two teenage boys.

Involving teenagers as Sunday school teachers is certainly one way of giving them the feeling that they have a responsible contribution to make to the life of their local church. However, the churches need to ask two fundamental questions about this practice. Is it being encouraged for the sake of the teenagers themselves, or because the churches are unable to recruit young parents and other adults into this responsible task? Have teenagers the appropriate professional knowledge and skill to take such a major role in the Christian education of young children?

The responsibility most frequently undertaken by teenagers after Sunday school teaching is that of leading other children's or young people's groups. This kind of responsibility is undertaken by very few (2%) of the teenagers under the age of sixteen, but by one in every thirteen (8%) of the sixteen to twenty year old church-goers. Unlike Sunday school teaching, this kind of leadership appeals almost equally to male (7%) and female (9%) older teenagers, and has a more even spread throughout the denominations to involve 15% of the Free Church members, 7% of the Anglicans and 7% of the Roman Catholics.

It is generally helpful to involve teenagers in planning their own youth club programmes and so on. Just 4% of the thirteen to fifteen year olds have become involved in this kind of youth club committee work, with the proportion rising to 10% of the sixteen to twenty year olds. Here again, boys and girls are equally likely to become involved, although their chances remain higher in the Free Churches (19%) than in the Church of England (9%) or the Roman Catholic Church (8%).

While the older teenagers are given an important role in Sunday schools and youth clubs, they are much less likely to become involved in bodies like the church council. Although, for example, in the Church of England young people are eligible for election to the parochial church council at the age of seventeen, just 3% of the older teenage Anglicans have become members of their parochial church council, compared with 20% who have been entrusted with Sunday school teaching. Similar responsibilities have been undertaken by 6% of the Free Church members and none of the Roman Catholics in this age group. Interestingly, the young men stand seven times as much chance as the young women of being among the small minority of teenagers elected on to their local church council.

If the Church of England's parochial church councils are unlikely to include many teenagers, the deanery synods contain even less. In the five geographical areas included in the survey and of the forty-two Anglican churches taking part, just four teenagers reported that they had accepted responsibility at deanery synod level.

As well as asking the young people to identify the posts of responsibility which they already held in their local church, the questionnaire also asked them to list the responsibilities they would like to hold, but so far had not had the opportunity. Once again, it was the responsibilities already held by a significant number of teenagers to which other teenagers were most attracted. For example, 8% of the thirteen to fifteen year old girls were already Sunday school teachers, and a further 24% wanted to become Sunday school teachers; 9% of the sixteen to twenty year old girls were already leading children's or young people's groups and a further 30% wanted to do so; 19% of the sixteen to twenty year old Free Church members were already committee members of young people's groups, and a further 34% were keen to join such committees.

Looked at from one perspective, there is much less desire on the part of teenagers to become members of their local church council than to become Sunday school teachers. However, viewed from another perspective, there are five times as many sixteen to twenty year olds keen to become members of their local church council (10%) than those already serving in that capacity (2%).

TOPICS

The teenage years are a vital period in the formation of attitudes and values. Young people can discover, develop and change their attitudes and values by talking with and listening to their friends and peers. To what extent do the churches give their teenager members the opportunity to discuss topics that are important to them, and which topics do they concentrate on?

In order to examine this question, the teenagers were asked to indicate the topics they had discussed in church groups within the past three months. The two topics most frequently discussed turn out to be highly religious issues, the bible (30%) and prayer (29%). At the same time, it needs to be emphasised that less than one in three of the church-going teenagers had actually been given the opportunity to discuss these central religious topics within the past three months.

A much wider range of issues concerned with politics, relationships and teenage culture had come under discussion within the past three months by between one in ten and one in five of the teenagers. In order of frequency, these issues include marriage (20%), the third world (20%), work (20%), personal relationships (20%), television (17%), the environment (16%), pop music (15%), unemployment (14%), law and order (13%), racism (12%) and sex (12%). Much lower down the scale, just one in twenty five of the teenagers (4%) had discussed such topics as the occult or religious cults.

Some issues are discussed with equal frequency by the thirteen to fifteen year olds and by the sixteen to twenty year olds. These tend to be religious topics, like the bible and prayer, or matters of popular interest, like television programmes and pop music. Matters of politics and personal relationships tend to be discussed more frequently by the older age group. For example, the proportions who discuss racism increase from 9% to 15%, marriage from 17% to 24%, sex from 8% to 16%, and work from 17% to 24%. Some topics, like marriage, personal relationships and the third world are discussed more by girls, while others, like politics, are discussed more by the boys.

Overall, the young people who attend the Free Churches have the most opportunity to discuss a wide range of issues, while those who attend the Roman Catholic Church have the least opportunity. For example, marriage has been discussed by 41% of the sixteen to twenty year olds who attend the Free Churches, compared with 23% of the Anglicans and 18% of the Roman Catholics. Similarly, the problems of the third world have been discussed by 51% of the sixteen to twenty year olds who attend the Free Churches, compared with 24% of the Anglicans and 15% of the Roman Catholics. There is only one exception to this pattern, and this concerns the occult. The Church of England seems to provide a much greater opportunity for its sixteen to twenty year old members to discuss the occult (22%) than either the Free Churches (12%) or the Roman Catholic Church (5%).

As well as looking at the proportions of the teenage church attenders who have discussed these topics at church groups within the past three months, those who had not had the opportunity to talk about these topics were asked whether they would like to do so. The replies to this question show that there is a great deal of teenage interest in discussing a wide range of topics, and at present this interest has not been adequately channelled by the churches.

More than half of the sixteen to twenty year olds who have not had the opportunity to talk about the following topics say that they would like the opportunity to do so: personal relationships (68%), sex (66%), marriage (65%), racism (64%), law and order (62%), the Third World (60%), work (57%), the environment (55%), unemployment (54%) and pop music (51%). Nearly half of them would like the opportunity to talk about the occult (49%), cults (49%), prayer (47%), the bible (43%), television (41%) and politics (40%).

The thirteen to fifteen year olds also show a considerable degree of interest in talking about a wider range of issues than their own churches have actually given them the opportunity to undertake. In descending order of importance, they say that they would like to talk about pop music (64%), television (51%), the occult (50%), work (48%), law and order (45%), sex (45%), personal relationships (44%), marriage (44%), the Third World (44%), unemployment (43%), the environment (40%), racism (39%), the bible (36%), prayer (34%), cults (26%) and politics (21%).

PRIORITIES

The kind of opportunities which the local churches provide for young people vary greatly from place to place. If the local churches allow the young people themselves to have a say in ordering the priorities of their church, where would the young people wish to place the emphasis? In order to answer this question, the young people were asked to say to which areas they would like to see their church give more time and how willing they themselves would be to co-operate in these areas.

The aspect of church life given the highest priority by these church-going teenagers emphasises the social gospel. 60% of them said that they would like to see their churches give more time to helping people in the local neighbourhood and that they would want to be involved in such a programme. The older teenagers give a slightly higher emphasis (63%) to this than the younger ones (57%). The girls give a much higher emphasis (70%) than the boys (46%). The Free Church teenagers (67%) give a higher importance to developing the social gospel than the Anglicans (62%) or the Roman Catholics (56%).

Second in their list of priorities, the teenagers place the role of their church in promoting their own personal and social development. 52% of them want more opportunity to share their thoughts, feelings and problems with each other in a Christian context. This priority is emphasised by 59% of the girls, by 38% of the younger boys and 46% of the older boys. The Free Church young people (67%) are more inclined to want their churches to develop in this direction than the Anglicans (51%) or the Roman Catholics (47%).

In third place comes the domestic concern of giving more time to learning what it means to be a Christian. This has a higher place on the agenda of the sixteen to twenty year olds (52%) than the thirteen to fifteen year olds (41%). It also has a higher place on the agenda of the girls (50%) than the boys (42%), and on the agenda of the Free Church members (60%) than the Anglicans (44%) or the Roman Catholics (43%).

In fourth place comes their concern with the Third World. Overall, 45% say that they would like to give more time to becoming aware of Third World problems. This objective receives roughly the same level of support from the older (46%) and the younger (45%) groups, more support from the girls (52%) than the boys (37%), and comparable support from the Free Church members (48%) the Roman Catholics (45%) and the Anglicans (42%).

In fifth place they locate their concern for learning about prayer and worship. This objective is important to 36% of the boys and 45% of the girls, to 36% of the thirteen to fifteen year olds and 47% of the sixteen to twenty year olds, to 58% of the Free Church members, 41% of the Anglicans and 35% of the Roman Catholics.

In sixth place they locate local ecumenism. The idea of spending more time co-operating with other churches in the neighbourhood is important to 31% of the boys and 45% of the girls, to 35% of the thirteen to fifteen year olds and 43% of the sixteen to twenty year olds, to 55% of the Free Church members, 43% of the Anglicans and just 30% of the Roman Catholics.

In seventh place comes the world-wide mission of the church. The level of interest in mission remains constant throughout the age range and does not vary greatly from denomination to denomination. There is, however, a significant difference in the level of interest shown by the two sexes. Thus, 22% of the boys and 41% of the girls say that they would like to become more involved in the church's missionary work overseas.

Far behind these other priorities in the eighth and ninth places come matters concerned with the church's outreach into the local community. While 60% of the church-going teenagers feel that they want to become more involved through their church in giving a helping hand in the local neighbourhood, only 17% feel that this involvement should stretch to taking a political interest in local affairs, and only 14% feel that it should stretch to include local evangelism.

The emphasis on keeping a low profile when it comes to political involvement on local issues is held consistently by both sexes across the age range and the denominational boundaries. There are, however, some interesting differences when it comes to the issue of local evangelism. Although none of the teenage groups are particularly enthusiastic about becoming personally involved in conducting evangelism in their local neighbourhood, there is more enthusiasm among the older group (18%) than among the younger group (10%); there is more enthusiasm among the girls (17%) than among the boys (10%); there is more enthusiasm among the young members of the Free churches (27%), than among the Anglicans (12%) or among the Roman Catholics (9%).

5 PUBLIC WORSHIP

At a time when the teenagers who attend church are very much in a minority among their contemporaries, it is important for the churches to listen to what these young people are saying about their attitudes to the public worship offered in their churches. Are they happy with what their local church is doing in its public services? Do they feel that these services are likely to attract other young people, and, if not, why not? The issues raised by this section will be reviewed under four main headings.

The first heading looks at the form of the *Sunday services*. Do the teenagers who go to church feel that the services they attend are generally boring, or full of life? Do they find the services relevant to their every day lives, and the sermons helpful? Do they really feel involved in the services, or do they feel that they are treated as spectators? Are they conscious of a barrier between the services of their church and their friends who do not come?

The second heading looks at the teenagers' attitudes towards *change* in worship. Do they tend to favour modern language services, or do they prefer the traditional language of worship? Do they like singing modern hymns, or would they prefer to stick to the old favourites? How willing are they to accept women ministers leading the worship of their church?

The third heading looks at the teenagers' attitudes towards the *ministers and priests* who conduct the worship in the churches they attend. Do they feel that their clergy are friendly people? Are they in touch with life, or old fashioned and out of date? Are they approachable? Are they good with children and teenagers? Do they listen to what young people have to say, and take the views of teenagers into account?

The fourth section looks at the teenagers' attitudes towards the *congregation* among whom they worship. How do they feel towards the older people in the congregation, and how do they feel towards the other teenagers who worship with them? To what extent do they find friendship within the church congregation, and is this friendship likely to cut them off from other teenagers who do not attend church?

SUNDAY SERVICES

All of the young people in the sample had recently been to a Sunday service, and for many of them this is their principal means of contact with the church. How positively do they feel about the church services they attend?

One of the main criticisms teenagers voice about things they dislike is that they are boring. An important danger signal to the churches is that more than one in three (37%) of the teenagers still in touch with the churches feel that the usual Sunday worship of their church is boring. This statistic is of particular importance, since many other young people who feel that church is boring have already stopped going anyway.

The proportion of teenage church-goers who feel that their Sunday services are boring is roughly the same among boys and girls, and across the age range from thirteen to twenty. There are some important denominational differences, however. These differences are most prominent among the sixteen to twenty year olds. In this age group, 47% of the Roman Catholics complain that their usual Sunday worship is boring, compared with 31% of the Anglicans and just 16% of the young people who attend one of the Free Churches.

The church which is not boring is the one which the teenager sees as being full of life. What proportion of the teenage church attenders feel that the usual Sunday worship of their church is full of life? Among the thirteen to fifteen year olds, just over a third (36%) feel this positively about their local church. A slightly higher proportion (40%) take the completely opposite view, and the remaining quarter (24%) are prepared perhaps to give their local church the benefit of their doubt. Among the sixteen to twenty year olds, again just over a third (35%) feel that the usual Sunday worship of their church is full of life. Among this older group, however, attitudes are hardening. A smaller proportion (17%) is willing to give their church the benefit of the doubt, and so the proportion rises to 48% who say the worship of their church is anything but full of life.

The denominational differences in the response to this question are once again important, especially among the sixteen to twenty year olds. It is the Free Church young people who feel most positively about the worship of their church, with 52% saying that their usual Sunday worship is full of life, compared with 40% of the Anglicans and 27% of the Roman Catholics.

The demand made by the young people is that the Sunday worship of their church should seem relevant to their daily lives. Only a small proportion (15%) of the teenagers who attend church feel that the usual Sunday worship of their church fails to meet this criterion. Moreover, this proportion does not vary according to age, denomination or sex. Although the older group is less inclined to feel that their church is full of life, they are not less inclined to think that it is relevant to their lives. Although the Roman Catholic teenagers are more inclined to think their church services are boring, they are not more inclined to think that they are irrelevant to their lives. Teenagers seem able to cope with boredom and lifelessness provided that the overall service seems relevant to their lives. Those who find church irrelevant have mainly stopped going.

The main teaching method used in the context of Sunday worship is generally that of the sermon. Sermons may present two kinds of problems for the teenagers, especially the younger teenagers. First, the model of communication on which the sermon is based is that of the lecture theatre. Since schools have largely moved away from this mode of communication, teenagers may well find it strange and, indeed, discover that they have never been trained to learn in this kind of way. Second, sermons are a form of mixed age and mixed ability teaching. Often they are aimed at the level of the experience of the adults in the congregation, rather than that of the young people. What, then, do the teenagers make of the sermons they hear when they go to church on a Sunday?

It is the younger teenagers, the thirteen to fifteen year olds, who derive least benefit from the Sunday sermon. Just one third (33%) of this age group report that they usually find sermons helpful. Another third (33%) are quite clear that as a rule they find the sermons in church anything but helpful. The other third (34%) say that it varies from time to time, but at least they remain hopeful that the preacher will say something that they can find helpful and to which they can relate.

Although there is not much variation in the response of the thirteen to fifteen year olds from different denominations to this question, the variation which exists provides some useful pointers. It is the young Roman Catholics who are most likely to say that they usually find the sermon unhelpful (37%), compared with 30% of the Anglicans and 28% of the Free Church members.

The older teenagers tend to find sermons more helpful than the younger teenagers. Among the sixteen to twenty year old church-goers, 46% say that they usually find the sermon helpful, compared with 30% who say that it is usually unhelpful, and 24% who say that it still varies very much from time to time. The denominational differences among the older groups are much more pronounced. Now it is clearly the Anglican sermon which falls into bottom place, with half (49%) of the sixteen to twenty year olds who go to the Church of England complaining that they usually find the sermon unhelpful. The Free Church sermon easily claims top place, with only 19% of the sixteen to twenty year olds who go to one of the Free Churches saying that they usually find the sermon unhelpful. The Roman Catholic sermon occupies almost exactly the midway position between these other two, with 36% of the sixteen to twenty year olds who go to the Roman Catholic churches complaining that they usually find the sermon unhelpful.

Not only is the teaching method presupposed by the sermon quite different from so much of the learning experience provided by today's schools, the whole environment of worship is often radically different from the young person's day to day experience. The emphasis in education is on participation, involvement and experience. Often worship is arranged as a spectator rather than as a participant activity. Even the formal rows of pews may tend to demonstrate this fact. To what extent do the teenage church attenders feel that the usual Sunday worship of their church treats them as a spectator?

Fortunately, few actually feel this way about their church, but interestingly the proportion increases slightly with age. While only 18% of the thirteen to fifteen year olds say that the usual Sunday worship of theirchurch treats them as a spectator, the proportion increases to 23% of the sixteen to twenty year olds. This increase is the same for boys and for girls.

The other significant difference is again between the denominations. The Roman Catholic teenagers are considerably more likely to feel that they are treated as spectators by their usual Sunday worship (26%) than either the Anglicans (15%) or the Free Church teenagers (13%).

The teenagers who go to church are taking part in something with which only a minority of their age group is familiar. To what extent do they feel that someone who is not familiar with the worship of their church could walk in and feel at home? How easy do they think it is for the stranger to join in the usual Sunday worship of their church?

Only a minority of the teenagers feel that it is really difficult for a stranger to join in the worship at the church, but this minority increases during teenage years. Thus, only 14% of the thirteen to fifteen year olds are aware of a real barrier between their church and a stranger, but his proportion increases to 20% of the sixteen to twenty year olds. The teenagers who attend the Anglican (18%) and the Roman Catholic churches (17%) are slightly more conscious of this kind of barrier than those who attend the Free churches (13%).

At the same time, however, one in three of these young people feels that his or her church is generally out of touch with young people today. This proportion remains constant with age and is roughly the same for both sexes. Again, there is quite a difference between the denominations. The Roman Catholics are most inclined to feel that the usual Sunday worship of their church is out of touch with young people (37%). The Free Church members are least inclined to feel this way about their church (21%), and the Anglicans occupy a position closer to the Roman Catholics (31%).

CHANGE

In the course of the years during which these young people have been growing up, the liturgy and worship of many of the churches have undergone some radical changes. For example, under the provisions of the Prayer Book (Alternative and Other Services) Measure 1965, the Church of England has been experimenting with a sequence of more modern forms of services (series 1, series 2, series 3 and series 1 and 2 revised) culminating in the production of the *Alternative Service Book 1980*. At the same time, a range of modern translations of the scripture have become accepted for reading in church, and changes have also taken place in hymnody.

These changes have not taken place without a great deal of controversy and conflict. In the 1980s there still exists a wide range of compromise within the local churches between the traditional and the modern. What do the teenagers who attend church make of this situation? Do they tend to be traditionalists who like the old ways, or do they tend to favour change in their churches? And how far are the churches they attend successful in meeting their attitudes on this issue?

Those who maintain that young people love the traditional language of the old forms of service receive very little support from the teenagers' own views on the subject. They give an overwhelming vote in favour of church services that use modern language. Just 7% of the sample say that they favour the services which do not use modern language. This proportion is the same for boys and for girls across the age range of the study.

Looking at the denominations separately, there is a slightly stronger lobby against the modern language services among the teenage Anglicans, but this still accounts for only one in ten of the teenagers who attend Anglican churches. Thus, 10% of the young Anglicans say that they prefer the older form of services, compared with 6% of the young Roman Catholics and 5% of the young members of the Free Churches.

It is often thought that church people tend to be more conservative about the hymns they sing than about the language of their services or their translations of scripture. It is argued that the music and words of the great hymns of the past draw strong emotional attachment. While a number of modern hymns have been incorporated into school hymn books, many of the well-known and well-loved hymns of the past continue to stand side by side with the new hymns of the twentieth century. Are the teenagers who attend church any more conservative in their taste in hymns than in their taste for modern language services?

Although there is overall slightly more feeling against modern hymns (14%) than against modern language services (7%), the vast majority of the teenagers who go to church are quite clear that they favour the use of modern hymns in the services they attend. The minority who come out in favour of sticking to the old hymns include more boys (19%) than girls (10%) and more Roman Catholics (17%) than Free Church (10%) or Anglicans (12%).

If the overwhelming vote of the young people is in favour of modern language services and modern hymns, how far do they feel that their preferences are being met by their local church? The answer is that just over a third (36%) of the young people feel that the usual Sunday worship of their church could be called modern. This proportion remains remarkably constant across the age range, for both sexes, and for the different denominations. The teenagers who attend church are much more in favour of the modernisation of worship than their churches themselves. This may have profound implications for the involvement of teenagers in the life of their church.

To what extent do the teenagers who favour modern worship, and yet find that their own church favours something less modern than they would like, blame the older members of the congregation for this disparity? Between one-quarter and one-third of the teenagers criticise the older people in their church for refusing to accept change. The sixteen to twenty year olds (31%) are more critical than the thirteen to fifteen year olds (26%). The Anglicans are slightly more critical (32%) than the others (27%). By way of comparison, only 3% of the teenagers feel that their contemporaries in the congregation would refuse to accept change.

Before leaving the analysis of the extent to which teenage church-goers would welcome change in the worship of their church, there is one other central issue which still divides the modernists from the traditionalists in many denominations. This concerns the place of women ministers or priests. What proportion of the teenage church-goers are for women priests and what proportion are against them? Their views on this issue are clearly related to their age, their sex and their denominational background.

It is the Roman Catholic teenagers who are most clearly against women having a place in the church's ministry, and their view on this issue does not change much with age. 25% of the Roman Catholic thirteen to fifteen year olds are in favour of women priests, and so are 27% of the sixteen to twenty year olds. 46% of the Roman Catholic thirteen to fifteen year olds are against women priests and so are 49% of the sixteen to twenty year olds. 29% of the Roman Catholic thirteen to fifteen year olds and 24% of the sixteen to twenty year olds have not yet made up their minds on the issue. So, in effect, this means that the older group are slightly more certain where they stand in the controversy, but that their views polarise in roughly the same proportions as the younger group.

It is the Free Church teenagers who are most clearly in favour of women having a place in the church's ministry. This, of course, is well in line with the traditions of many of the Free Churches. However, the view of the Free Church teenagers is by no means unanimous on this issue, although it does become clearer with age. Nearly half (48%) of the Free Church thirteen to fifteen year olds are clearly in favour of women ministers, and this proportion rises to nearly two-thirds (62%) among the sixteen to twenty year olds. A third (34%) of the Free Church thirteen to fifteen year olds say that they have not come to a clear opinion on this issue, and this proportion falls to a fifth (20%) among the sixteen to twenty year olds. This means that 18% of both age groups of the teenagers who belong to one of the Free Churches stand out against women ministers.

While the positions of the Roman Catholic Church and the Free Churches are relatively clear on the issue of women ministers, the situation in the Church of England is that there are pressure groups on both sides of the issue. Some overseas churches within the Anglican Communion have already begun to ordain women to the priesthood, while others, like the Anglican Church in England, do not as yet ordain women to the priesthood. More than half of the teenage Anglicans in the sample are in favour of women priests. The proportion rises from 49% of the thirteen to fifteen year olds to 54% of the sixteen to twenty year olds.

Among the thirteen to fifteen year old Anglicans, 17% are clearly against women priests and the remaining 34% have not made up their minds on this issue. The sixteen to twenty year old Anglicans are much clearer about where they stand in the controversy. The proportion of those who have not made up their minds falls to 19%. It is the anti-women priest lobby which gains most from this swing, bringing the proportion of sixteen to twenty year old Anglicans clearly against women priests to one in every four (27%).

How much is the place of women in the ministry a feminist issue among teenage church-goers and likely to cause a sharp divide of opinion among boys and girls? Although there is a significant difference between the views of the boys and the girls on this issue it is by no means a clear cut difference. Overall 31% of the girls and 38% of the boys hold out against women ministers or priests.

MINISTERS AND PRIESTS

The clergy have a central part to play in the public worship of most churches. The more clerically dominated the worship of the church, the more important it is that the clergyman is liked and respected by the worshippers. Often a church is judged on the ability of the minister or priest to be a good preacher, a good celebrant, a good pastor. What kind of image do these church-going teenagers have of the minister or priest who has the responsibility for leading the usual Sunday worship in their own church?

One of the main characteristics which the young people are looking for in their clergy is friendliness. First and foremost they need to recognise in the minister a humanity - a humanity which is approachable and accepting. Unless the minister passes this test, he will remain a remote and isolated figure. The majority of the teenagers in the sample give their clergy full marks at the first hurdle. Overall, only 3% of the young people positively feel that the minister or priest of their church is an unfriendly person, while another 5% have enough reservations about their minister not to be able to say that he is really friendly. Looked at in greater detail, 98% of the Free Church teenagers, 94% of the

Anglicans and 90% of the Roman Catholics say that the minister or priest of their church is a friendly person.

Friendliness is a very important characteristic, but by itself it is not enough to commend the clergy to their teenage congregation. They need also to be thought of as being in touch with the world in which the teenager is living his or her daily life. Again the majority of the teenagers feel that their clergy pass this test as well. This time just 10% of the teenagers feel that their clergy are out of touch with life, and 14% feel that their clergy are old-fashioned. To avoid the teenagers' criticisms of being old-fashioned or out of touch with life is no mean accolade. Again, it is the Roman Catholic clergy who are most likely to come in for criticism on this issue. For example, among the sixteen to twenty year olds, 14% of the Roman Catholics say that their priest is out of touch with life, compared with 4% of the Anglicans and 5% of the Free Church members.

If the clergy pass the first hurdle of friendliness with flying colours, and the second hurdle of being up to date only slightly scathed, they are somewhat more inclined to fall at the third hurdle of approachability. About three out of every four of the church-going teenagers feel that the minister or priest of their church is someone they can approach, but the other one out of every four has reservations about this.

A comparison of the responses of the different groups of teenagers provides some useful insights into the approachability of the clergy. More of the older teenagers (78%) find their clergy approachable than the younger teenagers (73%). More of the boys (80%) find their clergy approachable than the girls (73%). More of the Free Church teenagers (80%) find their clergy approachable than the Roman Catholics (74%), with the Anglicans occupying a midway position (76%). Those least likely to find their clergy approachable are the young Roman Catholic girls, while those most likely are the older Free Church boys.

The work of the clergy involves them in tackling a wide range of different jobs and working among a wide age range of people, from cradle to grave. It would not be unreasonable to expect some clergy to seem to be more at home than others working among children and young people. It is important, then, to examine the way in which teenage church-goers themselves rate the success of their clergy in their children's work and youth work.

Once again, the majority of the teenagers are complimentary of the ability of their clergy. 76% of the sample feel that their minister or priest is good with teenagers and a slightly higher proportion (81%) say that their minister or priest is good with younger children. These percentages remain roughly the same for boys and girls across the age range. There remain, however, significant denominational differences, according to which the Free Church ministers have the most favourable image and the Roman Catholic priests the least favourable image. For example, 83% of the Free Church teenagers feel that their minister is good with teenagers, compared with 76% of the Anglicans and 73% of the Roman Catholics.

Not only do the majority of the church-going teenagers feel that their clergyman is good with children and teenagers, they also feel that their clergyman listens to what young people are saying. Only a minute proportion of them, 3% of the Free Church members, 8% of the Roman Catholics and 8% of the Anglican teenagers, complain that their minister or priest ignores what young people are saying.

These statistics clearly indicate the important connection between teenage church attenders and a positive response to the clergy. At one level, these statistics can be interpreted as indicating that the clergy are generally doing a good job among young people. At another level, it needs to be borne in mind that it is likely that the teenagers who do not hold a favourable attitude towards their clergy may well already have ceased to be church-goers. On either interpretation, these statistics emphasise the seriousness with which the clergy need to take the development of their personal relationships with their teenage church attenders.

CONGREGATION

When teenagers share in public worship, they generally find themselves part of an all-age congregation. The usual age structure of a church congregation means that the teenagers are greatly outnumbered by older people. How do they feel about the congregation of which they are part on a Sunday? What kind of image do they hold of the older people among whom they find themselves worshipping? And what kind of image do they hold of their fellow teenagers in the congregation?

More than three-quarters of the teenagers who attend church feel that the adult members of their congregation are people who know each other and are generally friendly towards each other. Slightly fewer of the boys (75%) than the girls (79%) have formed this impression. The older group (74%) tends to feel slightly less positively about the adult congregation than the younger group (80%).

The difference of major importance concerns that between the various denominational groups. The teenagers who attend one of the

Free Churches (88%) are more likely than the teenagers who attend the Anglican Church (82%) to feel that the older people in their church are friendly to each other, while even fewer of the teenagers who attend a Roman Catholic Church (71%) feel this way about the adults in their congregation.

These denominational differences are not only reflected in the way in which the teenagers feel the older members of their congregation relate to one another; they are also reflected in the way in which the teenagers feel that the older members of the congregation relate to them. Thus, only 66% of the teenagers who attend a Roman Catholic church feel that the older people in the church are friendly towards them, compared with 82% of the teenagers who attend an Anglican church and 88% of those who attend one of the Free Churches.

Although three-quarters of the teenage church attenders feel that they are made welcome by the older members of the congregation, only one-third of them feels that this welcome actually extends as far as wanting young people to have a part in making the decisions which affect the life of the church. Just as the girls tend to feel that they are made more welcome by the older members of the congregation, so they tend to feel that the older people are more likely to let them have a part in making decisions. Thus, 31% of the boys and 36% of the girls say that the older people in their church like young people to have a part in making decisions. As they grow older, both the boys and the girls are less inclined to believe that the older people really want their voice to be heard. Thus, only 29% of the sixteen to twenty year olds feel that the older people in their church like young people to have a part in making decisions, compared with 38% of the thirteen to fifteen year olds.

Once again, it is the young Roman Catholics who feel least valued by the older members of the congregation. This is seen most clearly among the sixteen to twenty year olds, by which stage only 19% of the Roman Catholics feel that the older people like the younger ones to have a part in making decisions, compared with 37% of the Anglicans and 40% of the members of the Free Churches.

While one in three of the teenagers feels that the welcome given to him or her by the older members of the congregation might well extend to letting young people have a part in making decisions, only one in six of the teenagers believe that people of their age have actually had a real influence in determining church policy. 26% of the Free Church members, 16% of the Anglicans and 10% of the Roman Catholic teenagers actually feel that the thirteen to twenty year olds in their church have influenced church policy.

When teenagers attend church, it is important for them not only to feel welcomed by the older members of the congregation, but also to feel at home among the people of their own age in the congregation. Generally speaking, church-going teenagers see themselves as a friendly group of people.

It is the Free Churches which both attract the smallest number of teenagers and also stimulate the greatest sense of identity and friendship among them. The Roman Catholic Church, on the other hand, attracts the greatest number of teenagers, but stimulates the lowest level of friendship among them. Thus, 93% of the Free Church teenagers, 84% of the Anglicans and 72% of the Roman Catholics report that the thirteen to twenty year olds in their church are friendly to each other. Similarly, 94% of the Free Church teenagers, 89% of the Anglicans and 78% of the Roman Catholic teenagers report that the thirteen to twenty year olds in their church are friendly towards them.

From the church's point of view, it is important to provide opportunities for teenage church-goers to develop a sense of identity and a pattern of friendship within the worshipping community. At the same time it is necessary to guard against the development of exclusive cliques. How many of the teenagers feel that the church fellowship tends to isolate them from other young people of their own age? In fact, only a small proportion (3%) feel that the church fellowship isolates teenagers in this kind of way. Just three in every hundred of the teenagers say that the thirteen to twenty year olds in their church do not mix well with young people who do not come to church.

6 RELIGIOUS BELIEFS

So far we have looked in detail at the teenagers' patterns of church-going, what it means to them to be practising members of a church, and their attitudes towards the public worship which they attend. Our aim now is to examine more closely what their affiliation to a church means in terms of their private and personal beliefs.

In this chapter the term 'belief' is employed in a broad way to encompass four aspects of the teenagers' personal responses to their faith. The first section on religious *practice* examines the extent to which the public practice of their faith is also reflected in private religious practices. How important do these teenagers rate their religion in their daily lives? Do they pray, read the bible or say grace before meals? Do they want to study religion at school?

The second section on religious *experience* examines the grounds on which these young people base their allegiance to the Christian faith and their adherence to a particular church. What proportion of them talk about having had a religious experience, or the feeling the God has guided their lives? How many of them look back to a particular point of conversion in their lives? Given the fact the majority of the sixteen to twenty year olds in the sample have already been admitted to adult membership of one or other of the Christian denominations, to what extent have they experienced worship beyond their own denomination, within other Christian denominations, within sects and cults, or within the other major world faiths?

The third section on Christian *beliefs* examines the views held by the young church-goers on some of the central beliefs of the Christian faith. Is it necessarily the case that, because they are church-goers, they believe in God, or are we likely to find young agnostics, or even young atheists sitting in the pews next to the young believers? In other words do they all come to church to celebrate their faith, or do some come questing a faith which they do not at present share? What do they believe about Jesus Christ, the resurrection, life after death, and creation? How likely are they to believe that Christianity has a monopoly on religious truth?

The fourth section on *other beliefs* looks at a few of the beliefs which teenagers might hold and which some churches might regard as incompatible with the Christian faith. For example, do any of the young church-goers believe in reincarnation? Do they believe in their horoscopes, and so on?

PRACTICE

All the teenagers in the sample had recently been to a church service. Two thirds of them seem to try to attend church every Sunday, and only 2% of them attend a service less than once a month. One third of them also attend weekday services at least once a month. On the criterion of public religious practice, the sample indeed seems to represent a group of committed teenagers. But how important do they rate their religion in their personal lives and to what extent do they engage in private religious practices, like prayer, bible reading and the saying of grace before meals?

It is instructive to start with the thirteen to fifteen year olds. Among this age group, a little less than two thirds of the teenagers who go to church (62% of the boys and 67% of the girls) feel that their religion is important to them. One in four of the boys and girls (27%) say that they are not really sure whether their religion is important to them or not. 11% of the boys and 6% of the girls feel that their religion is of no real importance to them. Among this age group, it is the Roman Catholics (76%) who are most likely to feel that their religion is of importance, and the Anglicans (53%) who are least likely to feel that it is of importance. By way of comparison, 62% of the Free Church thirteen to fifteen year olds feel that their religion is important to them.

Among the sixteen to twenty year olds, the proportion of those who are uncertain about the importance of their religion has fallen from 27% to 18%. It might well be the case that those who are uncertain about the importance of religion in their lives have already stopped going to church by this age anyway. On the other hand, nearly one in ten (12% of the boys and 7% of the girls) of the sixteen to twenty year olds in the sample continue to attend church, but feel that religion is not important to them.

Among the older age group, there is still a little variation between the denominations, but this variation is much narrower than among the younger age group. The proportion of Roman Catholics who feel that their religion is important to them has remained constant at 75%. The proportion of the Free Church members who feel that their religion is important to them has now risen from 62% to catch up with the Roman

Catholic response of 75%. The Anglican response has risen from 53% to 67%, but it has done so only by losing a much larger number of its less committed teenage members than the other churches.

Private prayer is a practice advocated by all the Christian churches. What proportion of the teenager church-goers take this aspect of their commitment seriously? Again, the answer depends on age, sex and denominational background. The sixteen to twenty year old church-goers (51%) are more likely to pray every day than the thirteen to fifteen year olds (38%). The girls (48%) are more likely to pray every day than the boys (38%). The Roman Catholics (49%) and the Free Church teenagers (46%) are more likely to pray every day than the Anglicans (35%).

At the other end of the scale, nearly one in ten of the church-going teenagers reports that he or she never prays privately. This group consists of 10% of the thirteen to fifteen year olds and 8% of the sixteen to twenty year olds, 16% of the boys and 5% of the girls, 4% of the Roman Catholics, 12% of the Free Church members and 14% of the Anglicans.

The remaining half (47%) of the sample, who neither pray daily nor refrain from private prayer altogether, tend to pray irregularly and very infrequently. It is usually when something is worrying them and they feel in need of God's help, but most of them would not expect to pray as often as once a month, and certainly not weekly.

The different denominations place different levels of importance on the bible, and these differences are clearly reflected in the bible reading practice of the teenage members of these denominations. Daily bible reading is not an activity much enjoyed or practised by the thirteen to fifteen year old church-goers. Just 2% of the Roman Catholics, 6% of the Anglicans and 13% of the Free Church members in this age group read the bible for themselves every day. These denominational differences become much more pronounced among the sixteen to twenty year olds, when 41% of the Free Church members read their bible every day, compared with 16% of the Anglicans and 4% of the Roman Catholics.

At the other end of the scale, between one in four and one in three of the church-going teenagers report that they never read the bible privately. This group consists of 25% of the thirteen to fifteen year olds and 30% of the sixteen to twenty year olds, 23% of the girls and 35% of the boys, 19% of the Free Church members, 19% of the Anglicans and 37% of the Roman Catholics.

The remaining two thirds (63%) of the sample, who neither read the bible daily nor keep their bible completely closed, tend to turn to their bibles irregularly and infrequently. The majority of this group say that they read the bible just occasionally, but not as often as once a month, and certainly not weekly.

Saying grace before meals is a way of reminding the Christian of his or her dependence upon God, and of thanking God for his faithful response to that dependence. It seems that the practice of saying grace has become a very rare phenomenon among teenage Christians. More than half of the sample say that they would never think of saying grace, even on odd occasions. This is the response of 51% of the sixteen to twenty year olds and 55% of the thirteen to fifteen year olds, 51% of the girls and 57% of the boys, 41% of the Free Church members, 53% of the Roman Catholics and 60% of the Anglicans.

A further 36% of the sample report that they say grace occasionally. Again, in practice for most of them this means less than once a month. This leaves about one in ten of the teenagers who say grace nearly every day. This group contains 10% of the thirteen to fifteen year olds and 12% of the sixteen to twenty year olds, 9% of the girls and 13% of the boys, 6% of the Anglicans, 11% of the Roman Catholics and 23% of the Free Church members.

According to the 1944 Education Act, religious education is a compulsory subject for the timetable of every school. In practice, however, the actual provision made for religious education, as well as the content, varies greatly from school to school. Moreover, it is a subject which can attract considerable controversy and discontent among young people who are not themselves sympathetically disposed towards religion. If the teenagers who attend church could influence what happened in school, would they want to keep religious education on the timetable or not? Do they feel that pupils in school would be better off with religious education or without it?

The overwhelming vote of 80% of the young church-goers is in favour of keeping religious education in schools. A mere 7% feel that religious education should be removed from the timetable, while the remaining 13% vacillate between the two alternatives. There are no pronounced sex, age or denominational differences on this issue.

EXPERIENCE

Not only are most of the young people in the sample regular members of a church congregation, most of them have been admitted into full membership of their particular denomination. To what extent is their commitment to the Christian faith based on some personal experience of God in their lives?

About half of the sample feel that they might have had something which they would describe as a 'religious experience'. The nature of this experience can be very different from one person to another, but the important point is that half of the teenagers feel that they can look back in their lives and possibly point to something which spoke to them in a peculiar way of God's presence or activity.

51% of the sample are quite clear that they have never experienced anything they would call a religious experience. 22% are very tentative about it all, but feel that they might have had a religious experience, although they are not really sure whether that is the right description or not. A further 11% are more sure than this, but not completely certain. This leaves one in six (16%) of the teenagers who are quite clear that they have had a religious experience at sometime or other.

Religious experiences count most highly among the older age group, among the girls, and among the members of the Free Churches. 23% of the sixteen to twenty year olds are sure that they have had a religious experience, compared with 10% of the thirteen to fifteen year olds. Among the sixteen to twenty year olds, the girls (25%) are more likely to be certain of having had a religious experience than the boys (19%). The young members of the Free Churches (39%) are more likely to be certain of having had a religious experience than the Anglicans (21%) or the Roman Catholics (20%).

While half of the teenagers who attend church consider talking in terms of perhaps having had some form of religious experience, a much higher proportion (89%) talk in terms of having experienced God's guidance in their lives. Again the teenagers can mean a variety of different things when they say that they feel their lives have been guided by God. Some may have a dramatic incident in mind, while others may point to something much more ordinary or non-specific. The important point is that nine out of ten of the teenagers who attend church feel that they can look back in their lives and possibly point to the way in which God has influenced them.

Just 11% of the group are quite clear that they have never felt the guiding power of God in their lives. 34% are very tentative about it: they feel that their lives might have been guided by God, but they are not really sure. A further 29% are more sure than this, but they are not completely certain. This leaves one in every four (26%) of the teenagers who are quite clear that their lives have been guided by God in one way or another.

Like the reporting of religious experiences, the certainty of God's guidance is highest in the older age group and among the members of the Free Churches. This time, however, there is no significant difference between the boys and the girls. 34% of the sixteen to twenty year olds are certain that their lives have been guided by God, compared with 20% of the thirteen to fifteen year olds. Among the older age group, 47% of the Free Church members are certain that their lives have been guided by God, compared with 36% of the Roman Catholics and 25% of the Anglicans.

The greater emphasis of the Free Churches on some sort of personal experience of God is highlighted in the notion of a conversion experience, the point from which some Christians trace their true commitment to Christ. By the age of fifteen, 23% of the young people who attend one of the Free Churches claim that they have experienced something which they call a conversion. This proportion then rises to 49% of the sixteen to twenty year olds who attend one of the Free Churches. Thus, the conversion experience has become increasingly important to the late adolescents in the Free Churches.

By way of comparison, the notion of conversion is not something emphasised in the same way in the Roman Catholic Church. Just 14% of the young Roman Catholics feel that they have experienced a conversion and this proportion remains stable throughout the age range.

As far as the Church of England is concerned, some of the more evangelical churches emphasise the place of conversion, while other Anglican churches may never mention the notion at all. The personal experience of the young Anglicans reflects this ambivalence in their church. More of the young Anglicans say that they have experienced conversion than the Roman Catholics, but considerably fewer than the Free Church members. 17% of the Anglican thirteen to fifteen year olds and 22% of the sixteen to twenty year olds report a conversion experience.

As many as 92% of the sixteen to twenty year olds in the sample have already been admitted to adult membership of one of the Christian denominations. To what extent is the experience of these young people limited to within their own denomination, or to what extent have they experiences of other Christian churches?

Overall, it is the sixteen to twenty year old members of the Free Churches who have had the greatest experience of Christian ecumenism. Each of the young members of one of the Free Churches has attended on average worship in three denominations in addition to the one to which he or she belongs. The sixteen to twenty year old Anglicans are less ecumenically minded, although they, too, have attended on average worship in two denominations in addition to the Church of England. The sixteen to twenty year old Roman Catholics are the least ecumenically minded, having experience on average of only one other denomination in addition to the Roman Catholic Church itself.

Looking more closely at the figures behind these summary statistics, it emerges that the only denomination known to at least half of the young Roman Catholics, apart from their own church, is the Church of England. Thus, 51% of the sixteen to twenty year old Roman Catholics have attended a service in an Anglican church. By way of comparison, 22% of them have attended a Methodist church, 3% have attended a Baptist church, 3% have attended a United Reformed church, just over 1% have attended the Churches of Christ, the Salvation Army or a Pentecostal church, and less than 1% have attended and Orthodox church or a meeting of the Society of Friends.

The denomination best known to the sixteen to twenty year old Anglicans, apart from their own church, is the Methodist Church. Thus, two thirds (67%) of the Anglicans have been to a Methodist service. Next in line is the Roman Catholic Church which has been attended by 52% of the Anglicans. Baptist services have been attended by 28% of the Anglicans, United Reformed Church services by 22%, Pentecostal services by 11%, Salvation Army meetings by 6%, Churches of Christ services by 5%, Society of Friends meetings by 3% and Orthodox services by 2%.

The sixteen to twenty year olds who belong to one of the Free Churches have developed very close relationships with the Church of England, but much looser relationships with the Roman Catholic church. Nine out of ten of them have been to a service in an Anglican church, while only four out of ten have attended a service in a Roman Catholic church.

While most of the sixteen to twenty year old church-goers have been to services of at least one of the major Christian denominations other than that to which they belong, very few of them have had any form of contact with any of the other major world religions or with sects or cults. Just as the Roman Catholic young people were the least ecumenically minded, so they also seem the least curious about the other major world religions or about sects or cults. The young

Anglicans and Free Church members have had three times the amount of contact of the Roman Catholics with the other major world religions. Similarly, the young Free Church members have had twice the amount of contact of the Roman Catholics with sects and cults, while the young Anglicans have had three times this amount of contact.

First, we shall look at the major world religions in the order of the frequency with which they have been experienced by the sixteen to twenty year old church-goers. 6% of the Anglicans, 2% of the Free Church members and 2% of the Roman Catholics have attended worship in a Synagogue; 5% of the Free Church members, 3% of the Anglicans and less than 1% of the Roman Catholics have shared in Hindu worship; 3% of the Free Church members, 1% of the Roman Catholics and less than 1% of the Anglicans have attended worship in a Mosque; 2% of the Free Church members, 1% of the Anglicans and none of the Roman Catholics have experienced Sikh worship; just one Anglican has had some contact with Buddhism.

Second, we turn attention to sects and cults, again in the order of the frequency with which they have been experienced by the sixteen to twenty year old church-goers. 5% of the Anglicans, 2% of the Free Church members and 2% of the Roman Catholics have attended meetings of the Mormon Church; 4% of the Anglicans, 1% of the Free Church members and 1% of the Roman Catholics have attended meetings of Jehovah Witnesses; 2% of the Anglicans, 1% of the Free Church members and less than 1% of the Roman Catholics have attended Christian Science meetings; 2% of the Free Church members and 1% of the Anglicans have attended Hare Krishna meetings; 2% of the Free Church members and less than 1% of the Roman Catholics and Anglicans have attended the Divine Light Mission; 2% of the Anglicans and 1% of the Roman Catholics have had contact with the Children of God; less than 1% of the Anglicans and the Roman Catholics have had contact with Scientology or the Unification Church.

CHRISTIAN BELIEFS

At first glance, it might seem strange to ask young people who attend church whether or not they actually believe in God. On closer examination, this is really a sensible question. Their replies show that the majority of them (86%) are confident about their faith in God. On the other hand, 3% of the church-going teenagers are clear that they do not believe in God; at present they would classify themselves as atheists.

A further 11% of them are not sure about their faith in God; at present they would classify themselves as agnostics.

This implies that for every six teenagers who go to church in order to celebrate their faith in God, there is another one who attends in a more open ended way, either consciously questing a faith by which to live or for some other reason. Either way, it is important for the churches to recognise the different needs of the young people who are sure of their faith in God and those who are not. By ignoring the peculiar needs of the teenagers who are not sure of their faith, the churches could run the risk of alienating them further from religion rather than drawing them closer to it.

The pattern is for the young people who belong to the Roman Catholic Church to be surest of their faith, and for those who belong to the Anglican Church to be least sure. Thus, 91% of the Roman Catholics, 87% of the Free Church members and 79% of the Anglicans say that they are firm about their belief in God.

Traditionally, the central tenet of the Christian faith as defined by the ancient ecumenical creeds is the confession that Jesus Christ is the Son of God. To what extent are teenage church-goers still content to identify with this credal statement, and to what extent do they question it? The overwhelming majority of teenage church-goers (87%) are orthodox in their Christological language. They may well mean different things by that phrase, but they are showing little discontent with the formula itself.

A slightly higher proportion of the girls (89%) accept this Christological formula, that Jesus is the Son of God, than the boys (84%). A slightly higher proportion of the Roman Catholics (91%) accept it than the Free Church teenagers (89%), while the Anglicans show the lowest level of acceptance (82%).

Only 2% of the church-going teenagers reject the traditional Christological formula outright. The other 11% say that they are not sure about it. On the one hand, they are not comfortable with the idea, while on the other hand they are not comfortable with a straight dismissal of it.

The physical resurrection of Jesus from the dead provides a slightly greater stumbling block to teenage acceptance of orthodox Christian belief than the notion of divine sonship. While 87% of the teenagers are happy to say that they believe that Jesus Christ is the Son of God, the proportion falls to 77% who are able to say that they believe that Jesus really rose from the dead. This time, there are no overall differences between the two age groups or between the boys and the girls. At the same time, the same denominational trend continues to emerge, with 85% of the Roman Catholics and 81% of the Free Church members saying that they believe that Jesus really rose from the dead, compared with 67% of the Anglicans.

Once again, only a very small proportion (4%) of the church-going teenagers reject outright the physical resurrection of Jesus from the dead. The other 19% say that they prefer to keep an open mind on the matter and to be agnostic about it.

In Christian theology, the resurrection of Jesus from the dead is very closely linked to the doctrine of life after death. Among teenage church-goers there is considerably more scepticism about the doctrine of life after death than about the resurrection of Jesus from the dead. Life after death is believed in by just over half (54%) of the thirteen to fifteen year olds and just under two thirds (65%) of the sixteen to twenty year olds. There is no significant difference in the proportions of the boys and girls who hold this belief. Again, the familiar denominational trend emerges, with 64% of the Roman Catholics and 61% of the Free Church members saying that they believe in life after death, compared with 53% of the Anglicans.

While only 4% of the teenagers wanted actually to reject the resurrection of Jesus, 14% of the thirteen to fifteen year olds and 9% of the sixteen to twenty year olds stand out on the rejection of life after death. In order to complete the picture, nearly a third (32%) of the thirteen to fifteen year olds and just over a quarter (26%) of the sixteen to twenty year olds who attend church remain agnostic about the question of life after death.

One of the major issues of faith which continues to cause division among Christians of all ages is the extent to which, and the sense in which, biblical statements are to be regarded as true. An area in which this controversy is nicely displayed is that of the doctrine of creation. What do teenage church-goers make of the account in Genesis, according to which God made the world in six days and rested on the seventh? What proportion of them feels able to accept a belief like this, and what proportion wants to reject it?

This credal statement causes some fascinating divisions among the young people. In the overall sample, a little over one third (38%) accept the statement; another third (33%) reject it, and the remaining 29% cannot make up their minds on which side of the fence to come down.

The proportion of the young people who are content to accept the statement that God made the world in six days and rested on the seventh remains constant over the age range (38%). The change which does take place with age is a slight transition from agnosticism to rejection. Thus 36% of the sixteen to twenty year olds reject the belief, compared with 30% of the thirteen to fifteen year olds. At the same time, 26% of the sixteen to twenty year olds continue to sit on the fence, compared with 32% of the thirteen to fifteen year olds.

The sex differences on this issue are also interesting. The boys (42%) are much more likely than the girls (27%) to reject the statement. This is consistent with the theory sometimes advanced that boys tend to have a more 'scientific' outlook on the world than girls.

The denominational characteristics in response to this belief are most evident among the sixteen to twenty year olds. It is the Free Church teenagers who are most fundamentalist in their beliefs, with 48% accepting the belief that God made the world in six days and rested on the seventh, compared with only 19% who reject it. It is the Roman Catholic teenagers who are most clearly anti-fundamentalists, with 41% rejecting the belief, compared with 35% who accept it. Again, the Anglican teenagers find themselves in the middle territory, with 36% accepting the belief, 32% rejecting it, and the other 32% sitting on the fence.

Historically, the Christian churches have taught that Christianity is the only true religion, the only route to salvation. It is only comparatively recently that some Christians have undertaken true dialogue with other world faiths. How do the teenage church-goers feel about the exclusivity of Christianity? Overall, the old pattern of exclusivity wins, with 44% of the sample believing that Christianity is the only true religion, 28% rejecting that belief outright, and the remaining 28% being unsure of their own views on the question.

Again, it is the Free Church teenagers who are most committed to this position, with 64% of the sixteen to twenty year olds asserting that Christianity is the only true religion, compared with 46% of the Roman Catholics and 37% of the Anglicans of the same age. Conversely, it is the Anglicans who are clearest in their rejection of this belief, with 36% of the sixteen to twenty year olds saying that Christianity is not the only true religion, compared with 29% of the Roman Catholics and 16% of the Free Church members of the same age.

OTHER BELIEFS

Recent surveys on religious beliefs have demonstrated that it is not uncommon for some committed Christians to mix with their Christian doctrine a whole range of other beliefs and superstitions. Sometimes the result might well be an eclectic mêlée which would horrify the clergy and theologians responsible for their Christian education. Are there any signs that the teenage church-goers in the sample have formed an attachment to beliefs from non-Christian sources?

The first belief to come under scrutiny in this section concerns reincarnation, an ancient religious belief firmly rejected by the Christian Church. At the same time, it belongs to a set of popular notions which attract attention and sometimes discussion among young people. How clear are the teenagers who belong to a church about their denial of such a heresy? The answer is that just two out of five (39%) of the young church-goers actually reject belief in reincarnation. Another two out of five (39%) are not sure whether to accept the belief or to reject it, and the remaining one in five (22%) actually believe in reincarnation.

The tendency to reject belief in reincarnation is stronger in the older group (44%) than in the younger group (35%). The tendency to reject the belief is also stronger among the boys (42%) than among the girls (37%). The denominational differences among the sixteen to twenty year olds are also highly interesting. The young Free Church members are the clearest about their rejection of reincarnation as a non-Christian belief, with 56% rejecting the belief and only 13% accepting it. The young Anglicans are the least clear about the way in which reincarnation fits into their pattern of their belief; 25% of the Anglicans accept the belief, 35% of them reject it, and 40% do not know where to stand on the matter. By way of comparison, 45% of the Roman Catholics are clear about their rejection of the belief; 20% of the Roman Catholics accept it, and 35% have not made up their minds.

The second belief to come under scrutiny in this section concerns horoscopes. The majority of popular newspapers print horoscopes daily, and many teenage magazines carry them as well. To what extent is belief in the power of the stars over human destiny compatible with the Christian faith? In other words, what proportion of church-going teenagers would also claim to believe in their horoscope?

All told, just one in six of the teenagers in the sample believe in their horoscope. This minority contains a larger proportion of the thirteen to fifteen year olds (19%) than the sixteen to twenty year olds (14%), and a larger proportion of the girls (21%) than the boys (11%). It includes 18% of the Anglicans, 17% of the Roman Catholics and 14% of the Free Church members.

The third belief to come under scrutiny in this section concerns the existence of intelligent life on other planets. This is an interesting issue because it is an example of one of those beliefs which fascinate people of all ages, and perhaps young people in particular, but regarding which there is no conclusive evidence one way or another. The power of this belief to catch the imagination is more than adequately demonstrated by the large output of science fiction in print, radio, television and films. What do these church-going teenagers feel about the possibility of there being intelligent life on other planets, and does this belief in any way affect their lives?

The first point to be shown from the statistics is that it is not an issue on which the young people feel any pressure to come to a decision. The largest proportion of them (42%) keeps an open mind on the matter. The girls (48%) are more likely to keep an open mind on the matter than the boys (34%). Of those who have come to a decision, the weight of opinion is on the side of there being intelligent life on other planets. 34% believe this to be the case, compared with 25% who deny it. The denominational difference is again significant, with 36% of the Anglicans and 34% of the Roman Catholics accepting the belief in intelligent life on other planets, compared with 25% of the Free Church members. This is consistent with the pattern of Free Church members being more sure than the others about which beliefs count as a central part of their Christian faith and which do not.

Although one in three of the teenagers accepts belief in intelligent life on other planets, only a few of them consider that this intelligent life is likely in any way to interfere with life on earth. Just 7% say that they are concerned about the possibility of an invasion from outer space. Moreover, the largest proportion of the group (72%) does not keep an open mind on the matter, but rejects it out of hand. Science fiction may be fun, but these young people do not generally allow the ideas it generates to take a hold on their lives.

7 MORAL ATTITUDES

Traditionally, morality and religion have gone hand in hand. Historically, the churches have been firm in their moral teaching. Some have gone so far as to assert that religion provides the only sound underpinning for morality. On the other hand, a great deal of social research has indicated that sometimes religion does not really have the expected influence on the moral values, standards and behaviour of religious people.

Against this kind of background, it is of considerable interest and importance to ask precisely what are the moral values, standards and attitudes of the teenagers attending church today? How important are moral values to them, and is the morality they value the same morality as their churches believe that they are teaching them to uphold?

Only a handful (4%) of the teenagers who attend church dismiss the idea that moral values are of importance to their lives. The actual importance they attach to moral values also increases significantly with age. Among the thirteen to fifteen year olds, although only 4% actually reject the importance of moral values, a further 38% say that they are not really sure how important moral values are to their lives, leaving 58% who unequivocally affirm the importance of moral values. Among the sixteen to twenty year olds, the picture shifts so that, while 3% still reject the importance of moral values, the proportion who say that they are not really sure how important moral values are to their lives falls to 14%, leaving 83% who unambiguously affirm their importance.

But what do these teenagers who affirm that moral values are important to them actually mean by it? In order to throw light on this question, the present chapter proposes to review six key dimensions of these teenagers' moral attitudes. The first section looks at their views on *sex*, concentrating on the three topics of contraception, sex outside marriage and homosexuality. The second section examines their views on *drink and drugs*. The third section on *life and death* reviews their attitudes towards the sanctity of human life, through issues like abortion, euthansia and war.

The fourth section on *social trends* invites the young people to comment on the way they feel about the prevailing moral climate of the society in which they live. How do they regard society's attitude towards such issues as divorce, pornography and violence? The fifth section is concerned with *law breaking behaviour*. The young people are asked to assess their reaction to three violations of the law: parking in a no waiting area, travelling on public transport without buying a ticket, and the sale of cigarettes to children under the legal age. The final section is concerned with assessing the young church-goers' *integrity*. Psychologically speaking, this is a complex notion intended to evaluate how insightful the young people are into their own moral behaviour and feelings, and how willing they are to speak the truth about themselves.

SEX

It was the set of questions concerned with sex which caused the greatest nervousness towards the questionnaire among some of the churches, resulting in the design of a modified questionnaire for use among the under sixteen year olds. There is no doubt that a large proportion of the thirteen to fifteen year olds have already formed clear views on their moral attitudes towards these matters of sexuality. It is unfortunate that the churches were unwilling to look at what this age group is saying about topics of such central importance to their adolescent development. This is especially so since, as can be inferred from the replies of the older group, their developing views might well come into conflict with the expectations and teachings of their churches, with all the conflicting guilt this can produce in some young teenagers.

The ready availability of safe and reliable methods of contraception has helped to facilitate a revolution in society's attitudes towards sexuality. The churches have not been slow to debate the implications of such a revolution and to issue their recommendations. It is the Roman Catholic Church which has taken the hardest line on the matter and ruled firmly against the use of contraceptive measures. How do the young Christians feel about this central question, and are young Roman Catholics likely to take a very different stand from their contemporaries who belong to one of the other churches?

The majority view of these young Christians is clearly in favour of the acceptability of contraception. Overall, only one in ten of the sixteen to twenty year olds believe that contraception is wrong. The boys in the sample (15%) were twice as likely to take this conservative view as the girls (8%). Although there are some significant differences between the denominational groups, these differences are not very large. 15% of the

Roman Catholics consider that contraception is wrong, compared with 7% of the Free Church teenagers and 4% of the Anglicans. The difference between the response of the Roman Catholics and the other denominations is also seen in the fact that a slightly higher proportion of the Roman Catholics (16%) have not firmly made up their minds on this issue, compared with 13% of the Free Church members and 10% of the Anglicans. This suggests that a slightly higher proportion of the Roman Catholic teenagers have not come to terms with resolving the conflict between the teaching of their church and the prevailing views of the culture in which they live.

In order to complete the picture, it is 69% of the Roman Catholics, 80% of the Free Church members and 86% of the Anglicans who unambiguously reject the suggestion that contraception is wrong.

Second, we turn attention from contraception to sexual intercourse outside marriage. Traditional Christian teaching has been clear about confining sexual intercourse to the marriage relationship. Wider society has taken a much more liberal view. How do young Christians feel about this tension between the traditional conservative teaching of the churches and the more liberal views of contemporary society?

The teenagers' response to this question is by no means as clear cut as their response to the question about contraception. The majority vote of half (50%) of the sixteen to twenty year olds comes down on the liberal side of the fence. However, a significant minority vote of a third (35%) comes down on the conservative side, while the remaining 15% sit in the middle. The responses of the boys and the girls in the sample follow the same basic pattern.

On the question of contraception it was the young Roman Catholics who, following the teaching of their church, were more likely to adopt a conservative attitude. On the question of sex outside marriage, it is the young members of the Free Churches who are without doubt most conservative. 55% of the Free Church members claim that it is wrong to have sex outside marriage, compared with 32% of the Roman Catholics and 28% of the Anglicans.

Finally, we turn attention from heterosexual relationships to homosexuality. This is another issue to which the Christian churches have given considerable attention. Again, the traditional Christian standpoint has been to rule against homosexual practices. At the same time, as a number of surveys demonstrate, the liberalisation of the sexual attitudes of society at large has not led to such widespread acceptance of homosexual freedom as of heterosexual freedom. So, how do the views of the teenage church-goers on homosexuality compare with their views on, for example, the acceptability of sex outside marriage?

On both issues there is a wide divergence of opinion among the young people in the sample. However, the differences in the emphases of their responses to the two questions are considerable. First, a larger proportion (27%) of the young people are ambivalent or uncertain about their attitude towards homosexuality than towards sex outside marriage (15%). A larger proportion of them have clearly failed to make up their minds. Second, of those who have made up their minds about sex outside marriage, two out of five said that it was wrong, and three out of five said that it was not wrong. The weight of opinion is in the liberal direction. Of those who have made up their minds about homosexuality, three out of five say that it is wrong, and two out of five say that it is not wrong. The weight of opinion is in the conservative direction.

The third difference concerns the variation between the sexes. The responses of the boys and girls followed basically the same pattern in relationship to the question about sex outside marriage. Their responses differ considerably in relationship to the question about homosexuality. The girls are much more likely to keep an open mind on homosexuality (31%) than the boys (21%). The boys are much more likely to condemn homosexuality (56%) than the girls (33%).

Inspite of these three important differences, the denominational pattern remains in the same direction for both issues, although the pattern is less pronounced on the homosexuality question. The Free Church members remain the most conservative, with 54% of them ruling against homosexuality, compared with 40% of the Anglicans and 40% of the Roman Catholics.

DRINK AND DRUGS

A considerable amount of attention is given to teenage drinking habits and to experimentation with drugs. While the churches did not object to the under sixteen year olds being asked about their attitudes towards the more socially acceptable alcohol, they did object to the inclusion of questions about drugs. This means that we can discover from this study what both age groups think about drink, but only what the older group thinks about drugs.

The social acceptability of drinking is something which increases with age more rapidly among boys than girls. While 41% of the thirteen to fifteen year old boys consider that it is wrong to become drunk, the proportion falls to 33% of the male sixteen to twenty year olds. Coincident with this movement, the proportion of the boys who consider that it is acceptable to become drunk increases from 38% to 46%. Throughout the age range, one in five of the boys (21%) remain uncertain about their attitudes towards drunkenness. By way of contrast, the proportion of the girls who think that it is wrong to become drunk remains stable across the age range, between 41% and 43%.

Historically, it has been the Free Churches which have stood out most strongly against alcohol. This tendency is still clearly reflected in the attitudes of the teenage members of the Free Churches. The overall tendency is for attitudes towards this issue to liberalise with age. Thus 43% of the Anglican thirteen to fifteen year olds think that it is wrong to become drunk, compared with 31% of the Anglican sixteen to twenty year olds. A similar trend occurs among the Roman Catholic teenagers, from 36% to 29%. Already more of the Free Church thirteen to fifteen year olds consider that it is wrong to become drunk (49%) than their Anglican (43%) or Roman Catholic (36%) contemporaries. Then, instead of following the trend towards greater liberalisation with age, the Free Church members move in the opposite direction, so that two thirds (66%) of the Free Church sixteen to twenty year olds take a decisive stand against drunkenness.

The teenage church-goers in the sample adopt a much more conservative attitude towards drugs like marijuana than towards alcohol. On the issue of alcohol abuse, the sixteen to twenty year olds divided into two equal camps, with two out of five (39%) finding drunkenness acceptable and another two out of five (39%) finding drunkenness unacceptable. The other 22% had not formed a firm opinion on the matter. On the issue of the use of marijuana, quite a different division takes place, with more than three out of five (63%) finding it unacceptable and less than one in five (18%) finding it acceptable. This time, it is 18% who have not formed a firm opinion on the matter.

The same sex and denominational differences emerge among the sixteen to twenty year olds to the question of marijuana as to the question of alcohol abuse. The girls (66%) are more likely to judge the use of marijuana as wrong than the boys (58%). The Free Church teenagers are much more likely to stand out against the use of marijuana (84%) than the Anglicans (64%) or the Roman Catholics (56%).

LIFE AND DEATH

Christian teaching has always been at pains to maintain the inviolable sanctity of human life. Murder has been seen as one of the worst crimes against both God and man. The churches have never debated the acceptability of murder itself, but they have looked in detail at some of the issues which they consider neighbours to it. Can killing be justified in times of war; can there be such a thing as a just war or a righteous war? Are those involved in abortions guilty of murder, or are there situations in which abortion is the less of two evils, or can a time limit be set before which the foetus need not be regarded as an independent human life? Is it acceptable to allow the incurably diseased, the severely injured, or the very old and frail to die when life support systems might prolong their grasp on life, or even to hasten their death should they explicitly desire it? In short, is war, abortion or euthanasia necessarily morally wrong?

To begin with, the majority of young Christians today come out quite clearly on the side of saying that war is wrong. In every group of five, three (62%) are likely to say that all war is wrong, one (18%) is likely to say that all war is not wrong, and one (20%) is likely to sit on the fence or to say that there is something to be said on both sides of the issue. The girls are more likely to come out on the side of saying that all war is wrong (66%) than the boys (56%). It is not easy to discern a pattern in the denominational responses to this issue: over the whole age span from thirteen to twenty, 65% of the Free Church members, 62% of the Roman Catholics and 60% of the Anglicans argue that all war is wrong.

Abortion is another of those issues regarding which some churches refused to confront the younger teenagers, so replies are available only from the sixteen to twenty year olds. Again, three out of five (60%) of the young people in the sample come down strongly on the side of saying that they think abortion is wrong. One in four (24%) takes the other view that abortion is not wrong, and the remaining 16% had not really made up their minds. This time, the responses of the boys and girls are almost identical.

While there was no clear denominational pattern in response to the question about war, a very clear set of denominational differences emerge on the question about abortion. These differences reflect the stricter moral teaching of the Roman Catholic Church. Three quarters (74%) of the young Roman Catholics concur with the teaching of their church on this issue, a very much higher proportion than concur with their church's teaching on contraception. The remaining young Roman Catholics are evenly divided between 13% who are not willing to condemn abortion as morally wrong and 13% who are not sure which side to take.

The young Anglicans are much more divided on the question of abortion than their contemporaries who belong to the Roman Catholic Church. Almost equal proportions of the Anglicans say that abortion is wrong (40%) or that it is not wrong (44%). Slightly more of the Anglicans (18%) suspend their judgement on the matter than the Roman Catholics (13%).

It is the young members of the Free Churches who are most likely to say that they are uncertain about the issue (25%). Of the young members of the Free Churches who have made up their minds clearly on the question, twice as many (49%) are likely to judge abortion to be wrong as to say that it is not wrong (26%).

While some of the churches were unwilling to allow the younger teenagers to confront questions about abortion, they did not object to them facing a question about euthanasia. Their replies show that just over half (52%) of the thirteen to fifteen year olds believe that euthanasia is wrong, just over a quarter (27%) have no firm opinion on the issue, and the remaining 21% do not regard euthanasia as wrong. Between the two age groups there is a slight but significant movement towards liberalisation on this issue. Among the sixteen to twenty year olds, the proportion who argue that euthanasia is wrong falls to 47% while the number of those who argue against this view increases to 26%.

The denominational pattern identified in the responses to the question on abortion is reproduced in the responses to the question on euthanasia, although the contrasts are less marked. Among the sixteen to twenty year olds, the Roman Catholics are still the strongest voice in the anti-euthanasia lobby, with 55% of them voting against euthanasia, compared with 19% who vote in support of it. The Anglicans are again the most divided on the issue, with 33% voting against euthanasia, and 40% voting in support of it. The Free Church young people remain the most uncertain about where they stand on the issue, 35% of them adopting the position of indecision, compared with 26% of the Roman Catholics and 27% of the Anglicans. Of the young members of the Free Churches who have made up their minds clearly on the question, twice as many (43%) are likely to judge euthanasia to be wrong as to say that it is not wrong (22%).

SOCIAL TRENDS

Historically, the Christian churches were a powerful influence in determining the moral standards of society at large. With the present declining social influence of the churches, it has become much more likely that, on certain issues at least, the prevailing moral norms of society and the church's moral teaching may vary. To what extent do the teenagers who attend church themselves experience some form of conflict between their own moral views and the standards they find generally accepted by the society around them? Three interesting potential points of conflict concern social trends in divorce, pornography and violence.

As far as contemporary divorce procedures are concerned, there is only a minority of the church-going young people (15% throughout the entire age range) who feel that the present situation is acceptable. Among the thirteen to fifteen year olds, one in two (51%) say that they are concerned that divorce is becoming too easy to obtain, and one in three (36%) say that they are not sure whether divorce is becoming too easy to obtain or not. The sixteen to twenty year olds are less likely not to have made up their minds on this issue, and more likely to throw in their vote with those who are registering concern regarding the contemporary social trend. The proportion of sixteen to twenty year olds who are concerned that divorce is becoming too easy to obtain has risen to 61%. Among this older age group, the Free Church members register the highest level of concern (67%), compared with 62% of the Roman Catholics and 57% of the Anglicans. There are no significant differences in the responses of the boys and the girls to this issue.

Pornography is another of those issues expunged from the edition of the questionnaire prepared for the younger teenagers. The replies of the sixteen to twenty year olds demononstrate that, overall, there is almost as much concern registered by this age group about pornography as about divorce. All told, 56% of the sixteen to twenty year old church-goers say that they are concerned that pornography is too readily available, 24% say that they are not too clear about their views on the matter, and only one in five (20%) actually say that they are not concerned about the availability of pornography.

While the boys and the girls took a similar stand on the issue of divorce, they adopt significantly different profiles on the issue of pornography. Only 12% of the girls say that they are unconcerned about the availability of pornography, compared with 32% of the boys.

Looked at from the other perspective, 61% of the girls positively register concern about the availability of pornography, compared with 48% of the boys.

The denominational trends are more pronounced on the issue of pornography than on divorce. Concern about the availability of pornography is registered by 64% of the Free Church members, 58% of the Roman Catholics and 48% of the Anglicans. So, once again, the Free Church members emerge as the most conservative group and the Anglicans as the most liberal and accepting of social trends.

The general level of the social acceptance of violence on the television causes much less concern among the young church-goers than either the divorce-rate or the availability of pornography. 47% of the thirteen to fifteen year olds and 43% of the sixteen to twenty year olds dismiss the idea that violence on television is a problem at all. On the other hand, violence on television is registered as a real matter for concern by one in four (26%) of the thirteen to fifteen year olds and by one in three (33%) of the sixteen to twenty year olds.

Just as the girls are more concerned about pornography, so they are more concerned about violence: 38% of the sixteen to twenty year old girls say that they are concerned about the amount of violence on television, compared with 25% of the boys.

The denominational trends revealed by the young people's reaction to violence on television again place the Free Churches in the most conservative position, with 49% of the sixteen to twenty year old Free Church members registering concern. On this issue, however, it is the Roman Catholics (27%) who emerge as even more liberal than the Anglicans (35%).

LAW BREAKING

Our society is governed by a wide and complex range of laws. Some are self-evidently necessary and sensible, while others may seem tiresome, unnecessary or irritating. Every day many aspects of the law are ignored or violated. How do the young church-goers feel about their own responsibility to be law-abiding citizens?

Parking restrictions provide an interesting example of the kind of law that many adults will on occasions consider to be irritating. If there is no traffic warden in sight they will perhaps take the risk and park in a no-parking area or over-stay their period in a restricted-waiting zone. What proportion of the young church-goers will condone this kind of behaviour? It looks as if the law-breaking motorist will find little sympathy from the young church-goers, since only 15% of them are willing to disregard parking restrictions. A further 28% probably would not be too harsh on the offending motorist, but the other 57% are firm that parking restrictions should be strictly obeyed.

The girls (11%) are less likely than the boys (20%) to give positive approval to the breaking of parking laws. The Free Church members are the most likely to take a hard line on this issue (65%), and the Roman Catholics least likely (53%), with the Anglicans occupying a midway position (60%).

For many teenagers in the sample the question about parking restrictions involved a purely theoretical situation, since many of them were not old enough to drive anyway. The next question raises something much closer to the scope of their possible experience. What do they think about travelling on public transport without buying a ticket? What proportion of them would find this acceptable if they were sure that they could get away with it?

This move closer to the teenagers' own potential realm of experience does not result in a greater proportion of them being willing to flout the law. Only 13% of the young people condone the idea of travelling without a ticket, even if they knew they could get away with it. What it does result in, however, is a considerable reduction in the number of young people who say that they have not made up their mind on the issue. Travelling on public transport is sufficiently close to home for them to have thought about the issue and to have made up their minds where they stand on it. While 28% of the sample were keeping an open mind on parking restrictions, only 11% were doing so on travelling without a ticket. The net result is that travelling without a ticket is firmly condemned by 87% of the Free Church members, 74% of the Anglicans and 73% of the Roman Catholics.

The final question in this section draws attention to one of the laws which specifically restricts the freedom of young people. The law prohibits the sale of cigarettes to children under the age of sixteen. How do the young Christians who fall under this restriction feel about it? Are they, for example, any more likely to resent or reject this law than their church-going friends who are over the age of fifteen and, therefore, released from this restriction?

The answer is that the under sixteen year old church-goers are significantly more likely than those over the age of fifteen to approve of breaking the law which restricts them from buying cigarettes. However, even then approval is given to law-breaking behaviour by only 16% of the thirteen to fifteen year olds and 11% of the sixteen to twenty year olds.

It is among the older age group that the strongest denominational pattern emerges on the subject of selling cigarettes to children under the legal age. The sixteen to twenty year old members of the Free Churches are the most conservative in their outlook, with only 2% condoning the sale of cigarettes to children under the legal age. The Roman Catholics are the most radical in their outlook, with 15% condoning this behaviour. 9% of the Anglicans also take this liberal view.

INTEGRITY

It is usual for questionnaires designed to measure dimensions of personality or aspects of social attitudes to incorporate what is known as a lie scale. The original purpose of the lie scale, as its name implies, was to screen out the respondents who were not telling the truth about themselves or about their attitudes. However, the actual functioning of lie scales is much more complex than their original intention suggests.

Certainly lie scales can be of considerable help in assessing how many of the respondents are trying deliberately to cast themselves in a favourable light by failing to tell the truth about themselves. At the same time they can produce unique information about the respondent's integrity and their insight into their own moral behaviour and feelings.

The theory underlying the construction of lie scales is that there is a range of behaviours which are either both common and undesirable, or both desirable and uncommon. Those who are trying to create a good impression by failing to tell the truth about themselves tend to claim an excessive number of the desirable but uncommon characteristics, while denying the common but undesirable characteristics. How, then, do the teenager church-goers fit into this picture? How honest are they about themselves? What kind of moral integrity do they command?

The overall impression gained from their replies is that these young church-goers have a great deal of personal integrity and that only a handful of them, perhaps one or two in every hundred, have tried to distort the picture they present of themselves through the questionnaire. For example, the telling of lies is hardly regarded as a socially desirable characteristic, especially among Christians, and yet very few people, if any at all, can actually claim to go through life without ever telling a lie. The integrity of these young church-goers is nicely demonstrated by the fact that only 2% of them protest that they have never told a lie. Ironically, it is their acknowledgement of lying which can be accepted as a sure indication of their truthfulness.

Promises are made to be kept, and young Christians, perhaps more than others, might find themselves struggling to keep their promises. Yet promises are difficult to keep, and the majority of young church-goers acknowledge this fact. Only 13% believe that they have been successful in never breaking their promises.

Telling lies and breaking promises are activities which breach trust between people. The young church-goers are aware of the implications of such behaviour and acknowledge that they often fail to treat other people with the respect they deserve. Again, only 13% believe that they are not guilty of taking advantage of other people at some time or other.

Stealing is seen as a more serious matter than telling lies, breaking promises or taking advantage of others. Yet it is very easy for young people to take possession of something that is not their own. This does not necessarily imply thieving from local shops or from the family purse: it might be a pen from school or a coveted possession from a class-mate. The older they become, the less likely the teenagers are to deny that such incidents have entered into their experience. While just over a third (36%) of the thirteen to fifteen year olds maintain that they have never stolen anything in their life, this proportion falls to just over a quarter (27%) of the sixteen to twenty year olds.

It can be as socially undesirable to admit to certain emotions as to own up to certain behaviours. For example, jealousy has been regarded as one of the seven deadly sins. Yet, jealousy is one of the most natural of the human emotions. Do these young church-goers experience jealousy in themselves, and, if so, can they admit to it? The answer is that they know the experience and that they have the integrity to admit to it. Only 6% say that they are never jealous of others, and this percentage remains constant for the two age groups.

Resentment emerges as an emotion slightly less widespread than jealousy, and one over which the young church-goers seem to develop greater mastery with age. 15% of the thirteen to fifteen year olds and 22% of the sixteen to twenty year olds say that they no longer feel resentful when they fail to get their own way.

It is often far from easy to own up when one is in the wrong or to admit when one makes a mistake. Such behaviour is a major test of integrity. It is a test which about half of the young church-goers think they can pass. Their confidence in passing this test increases with age. Thus, 52% of the sixteen to twenty year olds say that they are always willing to admit when they make a mistake, compared with 46% of the thirteen to fifteen year olds.

So far, this analysis of the integrity of the young church-goers has taken into account age differences wherever they occur, but neither sex differences nor denominational differences have been mentioned. The truth of the matter is that sex differences and denominational differences hardly occur in this area. The only significant difference between the responses of the boys and the responses of the girls relates to the question about stealing. Girls (39%) are more likely to assert that they have never stolen anything in their lives than the boys (22%).

The denominational differences are not easy to quantify in a simple fashion, although they are very real. If the six items about telling lies, breaking promises, taking advantage of people, stealing, jealousy and resentment are added together to produce a scale of social desirability, the young Anglicans emerge clearly as the group most concerned to present a socially desirable image of themselves, possibly even at the expense of a little of their integrity. It is the young members of the Free Churches, on the other hand, who most clearly place integrity above social desirability or social acceptance. The young Roman Catholics occupy a midway position between the Anglicans and the members of the Free Churches: the young Roman Catholics are more likely to try to present a socially desirable image of themselves than the young members of the Free Churches, but less likely to do so than the young Anglicans.

8 POLITICS AND SOCIETY

For some, religion may be seen as an escape from the world, as a spiritual alternative to an involvement in politics and the problems of society. For others, religion may be seen as the complete opposite, as the spiritual stimulus for political activism and social reform. After reviewing the religious beliefs and the moral attitudes of the teenage church-goers, it is appropriate that we should turn next to an examination of their political values and their views of the society in which they live.

How involved are these church-going young people in politics? To which political parties do they give their support? How politically aware are they, and how passionately do they feel about the issues on which the major political parties hold opposing views? How socially aware are they, and how much do they care about the problems that confront their society and today's world? In order to attempt to answer these questions, the present chapter is organised in three main sections.

The first section looks at the support which the young church-goers give to the main *political parties*. What proportion of them favour the Labour party, the Liberal party, the Conservative party, or the National Front? How important is politics to them, and do they take an active part in political events? Have they any confidence that it makes a real difference which political party is in power?

The second section looks at the *political views* held by the young church-goers on a range of specific issues. What views do they hold on the debate between those who support nationalisation and those who support privatisation? Do they feel strongly one way or the other about the nationalisation of industry, or about private enterprise in health care or education? How do they evaluate the role of trade unions in an industrialised society? What is their attitude towards minority racial groups and to restrictions imposed on immigration?

The third section turns attention to the *social concerns* which occupy the young church-goers. How much interest do they take in the issues which confront today's society?

POLITICAL PARTIES

Generally speaking, it is impossible to separate political awareness from an evaluation of the major political parties. What kind of confidence, then, have these young church-goers in the political parties about which they inevitably hear so much from television and radio?

Unfortunately, the attitude inventory was designed before the emergence of the Social Democratic party, so that comparisons can be made only between the Conservative, Labour and Liberal parties. Overall, only two fifths of the church-going teenagers feel that they have confidence in any of these three political parties at the time when the survey was conducted. The other three fifths would not be sure about their vote along party political lines. The boys are more sure of where they stand within the party political structure than the girls. Both the boys and the girls become surer of where they stand as they grow older. In this way, 54% of the sixteen to twenty year old boys have confidence in one of the three leading political parties, compared with 46% of the thirteen to fifteen year old boys. Similarly, 34% of the sixteen to twenty year old girls have confidence in one of the three leading political parties, compared with 29% of the thirteen to fifteen year old girls.

Next, we focus attention on the support given to the individual political parties in turn. Overall, the Conservative party comes out on top, with the support of 17% of the church-going teenagers. The Labour party comes a close second, with the support of 14%. The Liberal party comes a poor third with the support of 7%. These averages, however, conceal some very important differences between the three denominational groups. These denominational differences are clearly present among the thirteen to fifteen year olds and then further emphasised among the sixteen to twenty year olds.

The old adage that the Anglican Church is the Tory party at prayer is in no sense undermined by the pattern of political preference displayed by the teenage church-goers. The sixteen to twenty year old Anglicans (26%) are twice as likely to place their confidence in the Conservative party as their contemporaries in the Roman Catholic Church (13%) or the Free Churches (15%). Similarly, the thirteen to fifteen year old Anglicans (23%) are nearly twice as likely to give support to the Conservative party as the thirteen to fifteen year olds in the Roman Catholic Church (13%) or in the Free Churches (15%).

Conversely, the Labour party draws significantly more of its support from the young Roman Catholics. 15% of the Roman Catholic thirteen to fifteen year olds place their confidence in the Labour party, compared with 9% of the Anglicans and 9% of the Free Church members of this age. Similarly, 19% of the Roman Catholic sixteen to twenty year olds support the Labour party, compared with 13% of the Anglicans and 11% of the Free Church members of this age.

The traditional alliance between the Free Churches and the Liberal party continues to emerge among the thirteen to fifteen year old members of the Free Churches. 13% of the Free Church adherents in this age group place their confidence in the Liberal party, compared with 6% of their contemporaries in the Roman Catholic Church and 6% of the Anglican Church. One in ten (10%) of the sixteen to twenty year old members of the Free Churches still give their support to the Liberal party, and now they have been joined by 11% of the Anglicans of the same age. Similar transference of allegiance to the Liberal party does not, however, take place among the sixteen to twenty year old Roman Catholics (5%).

The activity of the National Front among young people is a subject which attracts media attention from time to time. To what extent has the large proportion of otherwise politically unattached teenage church-goers been attracted to the National Front? In real terms, the numbers are small, but real seeds of attachment seem to have been sown, at least among the young Anglicans. 5% of the Anglican teenagers would claim to be attracted to the policies of the National Front, and so would 2% of the Roman Catholics and less than 1% of the young members of the Free Churches.

While only two out of five (39%) of the teenagers who attend church are willing to align themselves with one of the major political parties, an even smaller proportion, one in four (24%) feels that it is possible to become excited about politics or really involved in it. Overall, just 24% feel that politics is important to them. Nearly twice that number (47%) say that politics is certainly not important to them, and the remaining 29% are not sure whether it is important to them or not.

Just as allegiance to the political parties becomes clearer among the older group, so the importance they attach to politics increases (33%) in comparison with the younger group (16%). Among the sixteen to twenty year olds the Roman Catholics (36%) and the Anglicans (33%) are more likely to place importance on politics than the members of the Free Churches (26%).

Although a theoretical interest in politics may grow among the older teenagers, their active involvement remains negligible. Just 6% of the sixteen to twenty year old boys and 2% of the girls claim to take an active part in politics. Looked at from a denominational perspective, this small group of political activists contain 2% of the Free Church members, 3% of the Roman Catholics and 5% of the Anglicans.

To what extent is this lack of political involvement a matter of apathy or of political cynicism? The evidence seems to point towards a good deal of apathy, or at least to ignorance, as well as to cynicism. It is true that one in four (26%) of the teenage Church-goers are cynical about the value of party politics and say that it really makes no difference which political party is in power. However, this cynicism decreases sharply with age, so that only 21% of the sixteen to twenty year olds feel this way about politics compared with 30% of the thirteen to fifteen year olds, and never accounts for more than two fifths of the young church-goers who remain, as it were, the floating voters.

POLITICAL VIEWS

Given the lack of certainty which many of the teenage church-goers experience about their support for the major political parties, the lack of importance which they say that they attach to politics in general, and their lack of political activity, it becomes important to look in detail at their views on individual political issues. Do they in fact have firm views on central political matters, like the cases for and against nationalisation or privatisation, the role of trade unions, and the question of immigration restrictions? And, if so, do they tend to veer towards the left wing or towards the right in their political leanings?

Nationalisation is an interesting issue with which to start since debate about it causes a clear divide between Conservative and Labour party policies. This is clearly an issue which has been given minimal thought by the thirteen to fifteen year old church-goers. Two out of three (64%) of them say that they have not got a clue whether the nationalisation of industry is a good thing or not. A larger proportion of the sixteen to twenty year olds have given some consideration to the matter, but still 45% of them have not come to a conclusion one way or the other.

Among the sixteen to twenty year olds who have given thought to the matter, the weight of opinion clearly lies on the Conservative side of the fence, with 34% rejecting the nationalisation of industry and 21% supporting it. As is consistent with their party political allegiance towards the Labour party, the young Roman Catholics (26%) are more likely to speak up in favour of the nationalisation of industry than either the Anglicans (17%) or the members of the Free Churches (12%).

Two specific and rather different examples of the controversy between state control and private enterprise concern the place of private medical practice alongside the National Health Service, and the place of independent schools alongside the state maintained sector of education. While the issues of industrial organisation may be remote from the actual experience of the young church-goers, do they feel that they have any closer involvement with the questions of health or education?

Just as 45% of the sixteen to twenty year olds had failed to take a stand on the nationalisation of industry, so 42% of them have come to no firm opinion on whether private medicine should be encouraged or abolished. This time, however, the weight of opinion among those who have made up their minds lies on the Labour side of the fence. Only one in four (24%) of the young people feel that private medicine should be encouraged, compared with one in three (33%) who feel that it should not be encouraged. Even among the young Anglicans, a higher proportion (35%) vote against private medicine than in its favour (30%).

The case of independent schools is much closer to the hearts of these young teenagers than either nationalised industry or private medicine. On this issue, the proportion of sixteen to twenty year olds who have not formed a firm opinion, either for or against, falls to just over one in four (28%). This time, the weight of opinion among those who have made up their mind is five to two on the Conservative side of the fence. Only 20% of the young people feel that the independent sector of education should be abolished, compared with 53% who speak in its favour.

In order to assess the significance of these statistics, it is worth remembering that just 8% of the teenagers in the sample either were attending or had attended an independent school for the major part of their secondary education. It is clear that support for the independent sector of education is coming from a much larger proportion of the young church-goers than those who have had personal experience of it. It is also worth noting that the young Anglicans (62%) and the members of the Free Churches (56%) are quicker to speak in support of private education than the Roman Catholics (48%).

Strikes and industrial unrest are part of the climate of British society in which these teenagers are growing up. Depending from which side of the issue the matter is viewed, strikes can be blamed either on unreasonable management or on unreasonable trade unions. Five times as many of the sixteen to twenty year olds criticise the trade unions as support them. 63% believe that the trade unions have too much power, compared with only 13% who reject this criticism. The other 24% have not made up their minds on the matter. Again, the Free Church sixteen to twenty year olds (68%) and the Anglicans (67%) are more likely to be critical of the trade unions that the Roman Catholics (60%).

The final issue to be reviewed in this section is the controversial one of immigration restrictions. To what extent do these young church-goers believe that immigration into Britain should be restricted? Just one in five (19%) of them believe that immigration restriction should be lifted. This proportion remains constant across the age range and stands at roughly the same level for the boys and the girls. The denominational differences, as ever, are quite striking. The young members of the Free Churches take the most liberal stand with 26% of them voting against immigration restrictions. The young Anglicans take the least liberal stand, with only 13% of them voting against immigration restrictions. The young Roman Catholics occupy the midway position with 21% voting against immigration restrictions.

For every one of the teenagers who believes that restrictions should not be placed on immigration, there are three who believe that immigration should be restricted. This view is taken by 53% of the thirteen to fifteen year olds and 61% of the sixteen to twenty year olds. The question raised by these statistics is this: how do these young people who wish to insist on firm immigration restrictions feel about the immigrants already living in this country?

The answer to this question indicates that racial prejudice is far from being incompatible with church attendance. One in four (25%) of the teenage church-goers feels that there are too many black people living in this country. The boys (29%) are more inclined to be prejudiced in this way than the girls (22%). The young Anglicans are more inclined to be prejudiced (30%) than the Roman Catholics (23%) or the Free Church teenagers (18%). At the same time, it must be stressed that for every one church-going teenager who is racially prejudiced in this way there are two who are clearly not, and one other who is not sure whether he or she shares this prejudice or not.

While immigration restrictions might be conceived as one way of demonstrating patriotism, another way is through the support of home industry. While 56% of the young people are anxious to restrict immigration, only 36% are anxious to support home industry.

The 'Buy British' slogan is taken seriously by roughly the same proportion of boys and girls through the age range. What is of particular interest is the way in which the young members of the Free Churches, who were least likely to wish to restrict immigration, are also least likely to want to guarantee particular advantages to home industry. Thus, only 27% of the Free Church teenagers report that they would rather buy a British car than one made in another country, compared with 37% of the young Anglicans and 37% of the young Roman Catholics. The young Free Church members are clearly more likely to stand out consistently against forms of protectionism.

SOCIAL CONCERNS

From an analysis of their political views, we turn attention to an examination of the attitudes of teenage church-goers to the society in which they live. How much interest do they take in the issues which are discussed regularly on the television, on the radio and in the press? How seriously do they take world problems and the criticisms made of their own society?

To begin with, only a very small proportion of the young people show any real confidence in the direction in which world politics is moving. Day by day they hear of wars, conflicts and terrorist activities. They see news broadcasts of bombings, killings and destruction. They listen to the inability of international super-powers to come to an agreement on the deployment and limitation of nuclear war-heads. They hear of strikes, economic recessions, redundancy and unemployment. Against this background, only 13% of the young church-goers can say that they are not worried about the world situation.

Among the thirteen to fifteen year olds, the boys are showing more positive concern about the world situation than the girls. At this age, nearly two thirds of the boys (63%) are saying that they are worried about the world situation, compared with just under half 48% of the girls. This does not mean that the girls are feeling any more positive than the boys about the world situation, but rather that they are less likely to be sufficiently caught up in world matters to have formed any clear opinion about them.

Both the boys and the girls in the sixteen to twenty year age group are taking the implications of the world situation much more to heart that the younger teenage church-goers. The proportion of the girls who imply that they are disinterested in the world situation halves from 40% to 20%. The proportion of disinterested boys also halves from 25% to

13%. This means that among the sixteen to twenty year olds, 71% of the boys and 67% of the girls are registering concern about the world situation.

Two of the major threats to the world's future, which catch the imagination of young people and generate considerable concern in their minds, are the risk of nuclear war and the risk of pollution to the environment. Overall, 65% of the young people register concern about the risk of pollution to the environment, and even more (70%) register concern about the risk of nuclear war. Once again it is the girls who take these two problems more to heart that the boys, and the sixteen to twenty year olds who take them more to heart than the thirteen to fifteen year olds.

Looking first at the question of nuclear war, only 12% of the thirteen to fifteen year old boys have not formed an opinion on the matter; this proportion falls to 7% among the sixteen to twenty year old boys. In both age groups, twice as many girls as boys have not formed an opinion on the risk of nuclear war, that is to say 27% of the thirteen to fifteen year old girls and 17% of the sixteen to twenty year old girls. The small minority who are clear that they are not concerned about the risk of nuclear war consists of 12% of the thirteen to fifteen year old boys and 18% of the sixteen to twenty year old boys, 9% of the thirteen to fifteen year old girls and 13% of the sixteen to twenty year old girls.

The threat of nuclear war is something which is more likely to cause concern among the young Roman Catholics (73%) and the young Anglicans (70%) than among the young members of the Free Churches (62%).

Looking next at the question of pollution to the environment, there seems to be a little less urgency in the minds of the young people to become sure of their response to this issue than to the issue of nuclear war. Among the thirteen to fifteen year olds, 20% of the boys and 31% of the girls have not formed an opinion on the issue of pollution. Among the sixteen to twenty year olds, the proportion of the young people who have not formed an opinion falls, but not dramatically, to 18% of the boys and 22% of the girls. The small minority who are clear that they are not concerned about the risk of pollution to the environment consists of 10% of the boys from both age groups and 11% of the girls from both age groups. There are no significant denominational differences on this issue.

It seems, therefore, that the majority of the young church-goers are showing concern about the world problems, like nuclear war and pollution, which threaten their own survival. Do they show as much concern about the problems which affect other people, but only at a distance from their own personal experience and lives? For example, how concerned are they about the poverty of the Third World and the homelessness of refugees?

Only a very small proportion of the young people close their minds to either of these problems. Overall, just 9% deny feeling concern about the poverty of the Third World, and 5% deny feeling concern about the problems of homelessness. Homelessness is the more concrete of the two images, and this is responded to with equal passion and commitment by thirteen to fifteen year olds and sixteen to twenty year olds alike. Among both age groups, it is the girls who are less likely to sit on the fence and more likely to feel compassion and concern for those who are homeless. Thus, 82% of the girls register positive concern about the problem of homelessness, and so do 70% of the boys.

The thirteen to fifteen year olds find it less easy to identify with the poverty of the Third World than with the more concrete problem of homelessness. While 18% of this age group have failed to determine their level of concern for the homeless, 29% have failed to determine their level of concern for the poverty of the Third World. The sixteen to twenty year olds are more likely to be committed to the Third World, although 22% still fail to know where they stand on the issue.

On the question of the Third World, the girls once again show a higher level of concern than the boys, although the difference is not quite as great as on the question of homelessness. Among the thirteen to fifteen year olds, 62% of the girls and 56% of the boys register positive concern about the poverty of the Third World. Among the sixteen to twenty year olds this proportion rises to 75% of the girls and 66% of the boys.

The social conscience of the Free Churches is reflected in a high level of concern being registered on both the poverty of the Third World and homelessness, especially among the sixteen to twenty year olds. Thus, among this age group, 75% of the Free Church members are concerned about the poverty of the Third World, compared with 70% of the Anglicans and the Roman Catholics. Similarly, 88% of the Free Church members are concerned about the problem of homelessness, compared with 78% of the Anglicans and 74% of the Roman Catholics.

Moving closer to home, two issues which have been in the limelight of the media are inflation and unemployment. How much do these issues concern teenage church-goers today? The answer is that, overall, only 11% are unconcerned about inflation, and an even smaller minority (7%) are unconcerned about unemployment.

Inflation is a fairly abstract concept. One in three (33%) of the thirteen to fifteen year olds remains uncertain about what precisely the concept of inflation means to him or her. Most of the thirteen to fifteen year olds who have given thought to the concept contemplate it with concern. Five times as many of the thirteen to fifteen year olds (56%) say that they are concerned about the rate of inflation as those who deny concern (11%). Inflation is an economic concept which is more likely to cause concern among thirteen to fifteen year old boys (63%) than among the girls of the same age (52%).

Among the sixteen to twenty year olds, the proportion of the young people who have not worked out what inflation means to them falls by half to 16%. This leads to almost seven times as many of the sixteen to twenty year olds (74%) saying that they are concerned about the rate of inflation as those who deny concern (11%). In this older age group, inflation still remains more likely to cause concern among the boys (78%) than among the girls (71%), although the difference between the sexes has been narrowed slightly.

Unemployment is a more concrete concept than inflation, and the young people are more likely to have formed an opinion about the urgency of the problem at a younger age. On this issue, 23% of the thirteen to fifteen year olds and 12% of the sixteen to twenty year olds remain uncertain about what precisely the concept of unemployment means to them. Again, most of the young people who have given thought to the concept contemplate it with concern. Over seven times as many of the thirteen to fifteen year olds (68%) say that they are concerned about the issue of unemployment as those who deny concern (9%). Among the sixteen to twenty year olds, the contrast widens even further, so that fourteen times as many (83%) register concern about unemployment as those who deny concern (6%).

Unlike inflation, unemployment is a concept which gives rise to as much concern among the girls as among the boys. Girls may well show less concern about the erosion of the value of money through inflation, but they show an equal concern with the boys for those who are currently out of work and for their own predicament in the job market.

Being concerned about unemployment is one matter, but how much do the young church-goers actually understand the extent of the problem? For example, how do they view those who are actually out of work? Does the notion of the work ethic continue to persist so that to some extent the young people might tend to blame the unemployed for their own predicament? How much do they grasp the consequences of the effects of economic recession on job availability? Do they still believe that the work is there to be found, if people look hard enough for it?

As many as three out of seven (44%) of the thirteen to fifteen year old church-goers believe that most unemployed people could have a job if they really wanted. Two out of seven (28%) reject this belief and the remaining two (29%) feel uncertain about it. The sixteen to twenty year olds have become slightly more pessimistic about the availability of work, and yet still only 39% of them have come to believe that there are insufficient jobs to go around and that the unemployed are not to be blamed for their predicament.

The denominational differences on this issue are also of significance, especially among the sixteen to twenty year olds. 47% of the Anglicans hold the view that most unemployed people could have a job if they really wanted, compared with 34% of the Roman Catholics and 30% of the members of one of the Free Churches.

Economic recession, inflation and unemployment are coupled, in the minds of some, with decaying standards and rising social unrest. The young church-goers are obviously showing a great deal of concern about the issues of inflation and unemployment: to what extent do they also point to other associated problems?

The perceptions which people hold of the crime rate are a good indication of their feelings about the general direction of the society in which they live. Those who believe that the crime rate is rising tend to see themselves as living through an age of declining law and order, deteriorating social responsibility, rising unrest and increasing insecurity. Even among the thirteen to fifteen year olds, two in every three (68%) of the young people are living with the idea that the crime rate is rising, and this proportion increases to 74% of the sixteen to twenty year olds.

By way of comparison, less than one in ten (8% of the thirteen to fifteen year olds and 10% of the sixteen to twenty year olds) feel confident that they are living in a society in which the crime rate is not rising. The remaining 23% of the thirteen to fifteen year olds and the remaining 17% of the sixteen to twenty year olds keep an open mind on this matter.

The perceptions which people hold of the National Health Service are a good indication of their feelings about the general direction of the Welfare State. On this basis it seems that, as they become older, a growing proportion of the young people are disillusioned by the security offered to them by the Welfare State. Among the thirteen to fifteen year olds, 29% are showing concern that the health service is inefficient. Among the sixteen to twenty year olds, this has grown to 43%. Another 23% of the sixteen to twenty year olds are not at all sure about the wisdom of placing their confidence in the health service, leaving only one in three (34%) confident in its efficiency.

In summary, then, the majority of the young church-goers display a considerable level of concern about the problems which confront the world today. Is this the kind of concern which leaves them feeling helpless and hopeless, or do they feel that they can in fact do something about the situations which cause them concern?

Overall, twice as many of the young people (45%) feel that it is within their power to do something towards solving the world's problems, compared with those who feel they can do nothing (23%). The remaining 32% are on the touch line, neither yet convinced that it is within their power to do something, nor yet completely oppressed by the feeling of powerlessness in the situation.

Whether they perceive the problems facing their society accurately or not, there can be no doubt that the majority of teenage church-goers show a real concern about these problems. Whether they are realistic in their assessment or not, the majority of them remain hopeful and confident that they can make some contribution, however small, to helping to resolve these problems.

9 WORK AND LEISURE

For some young people, being a member of a church is a very central aspect of their lives, while for others their church membership is something of much more peripheral significance. In order to understand just where their church membership belongs within the wider context of their response to life, we need to examine two other aspects of the young church-goers' lives. We need to give attention to how they feel about their working time, whether this means time spent at school, in tertiary education or in employment, and how they feel about their leisure time. These two areas will be reviewed in turn.

The review of the young church-goers' responses to their working lives will enable us to assess the satisfaction they receive from their time at school or at work. It will enable us to assess their ambition and motivation, and the extent to which the work ethic is associated with church membership. What proportion of the young church-goers is likely to be coming to church as an escape from an unsatisfactory and unhappy working life?

The review of the young church-goers' responses to their leisure will enable us to assess the part played by their church membership within their overall use of their non-working time. It will enable us to assess the range of leisure and recreational activities in which they engage, and the extent to which they are satisfied with their use of their leisure time. What proportion of the young church-goers is likely to be coming to church because they have nothing else to do in their leisure time, and what proportion is likely to be giving their church membership a priority within a busy and fully-occupied life?

WORK

Chapter 3 has already examined in some detail what is meant by the working lives of the 1328 young people who responded to the attitude inventory. By way of resumé, all of the thirteen to fifteen year olds, were, naturally, still at school. Three fifths (58%) of the sixteen to twenty year old church attenders were also still engaged in some form of full-time education. 22% of them were in school, and 36% of them were studying at an institute of further or higher education, a technical college, a college of education, a university and so on. A further 10% of them had left full-time education to begin to earn a living, but at the same time they were involved in some form of part-time education, like day-release schemes. 26% of the sixteen to twenty year old church-goers were in full-time employment without simultaneously undertaking further education. The remaining 6% of these young people were unemployed. Chapter 3 also described in detail the wide range of jobs undertaken by the young men and women in this sample who had begun to earn their own living.

The first question which this chapter wishes to pose concerns the overall level of satisfaction which these young church-goers are deriving from their working lives. At this stage, I do not wish to try to compare the levels of satisfaction recorded by those in different occupations, or even to make a distinction between those still in full-time education and those earning a living. After excluding those who are currently out of work from the analysis, my concern is to identify how satisfied the young people are with whatever it is which occupies their working lives and accounts for a substantial proportion of their time. Are they happy with their working lives, or are they unhappy?

The statistics show that the vast majority of the young church-goers report that they are happy in their work or at their school. Just 5% of the thirteen to fifteen year olds and 7% of the sixteen to twenty year olds say that they are actually unhappy at work or at school. There is, then, little evidence to support the notion that teenagers turn to the church as an escape from an unhappy time at school or at work.

The small minority of the young church-goers who are unhappy at their school or at their work is evenly distributed between the two sexes and among the three denominational groups. The boys are neither more likely nor less likely than the girls to be unhappy with their working lives. Similarly the Roman Catholic churches, the Anglican churches and the Free Church churches are all likely to find the same small proportion of their young members suffering from an unsatisfactory school or working life.

Sometimes, young church-goers complain that their church member-ship isolates them from their peers at work or at school. To what extent is the unhappiness with their work or their school, which is reported by 5% of the thirteen to fifteen year olds and 7% of the sixteen to twenty year olds, associated with the feeling of antipathy between themselves and their peers? Again the answer is that very few of the young church-goers actually feel cut off in this kind of way. Just 3% of the thirteen to fifteen year olds and less than 2% of the sixteen to twenty year olds say that they dislike the people with whom they go to school or with whom they work. The vast majority of young church-goers thus seem to be well integrated among their class-mates or among their work- mates. This is equally true for the boys and for the girls, for the Roman Catholics, for the Anglicans and for the young members of the Free Churches.

Although the majority of the young church-goers are happy with their working life, whether at school or in employment, and like the people alongside whom they work or study, this does not mean that their working lives are not also a great source of tension and anxiety for them. Many more young people find that they worry about their work than do not worry about it. Overall, 52% of the young church-goers say that they often worry about their work, compared with 34% who are clear that they do not often worry about their work. The remaining 14% probably worry about their work from time to time, but not frequently enough to say that they often worry about it.

The younger teenagers (57%) are more inclined to worry about their work than the older teenagers (47%). The girls (55%) are more inclined to worry about their work than the boys (48%). Among the older teenagers this question begins to reveal a denominational difference which is seen more clearly in the next chapter on their well-being and worries. The sixteen to twenty year old members of the Free Churches are more inclined to deny worrying about their work than either the Roman Catholics or the Anglicans. Thus, 48% of the sixteen to twenty year old members of the Free Churches say that they definitely do not often worry about their work, compared with 36% of the Anglicans and 37% of the Roman Catholics of the same age.

Not only do the majority of the young church-goers enjoy their work, they also attach a lot of importance to their work, whether in school or in employment. The vast majority of the young church-goers are highly committed to the notion that it is important for them to work hard. Indeed, 94% of both age groups say that they think it is important to work hard. Among the thirteen to fifteen year olds, only 1% deny the importance of working hard and 5% feel uncertain about the issue. Among the sixteen to twenty year olds, 2% deny the importance of working hard and 4% feel uncertain about the issue.

Alongside their willingness to work hard, the majority of the young church-goers are highly motivated young people who want to do well at their work. Overall, 84% of the total sample claim to want to get to the top in their work, compared with just 5% who have decided that they are not concerned to be ambitious in this kind of way. The remaining 11% are undecided as to how ambitious they really are in relationship to their work.

The younger teenagers (87%) tend to be slightly more ambitious about their work than older teenagers (81%). The boys (88%) tend to be slightly more ambitious than the girls (82%). Just as the young members of the Free Churches are slightly less inclined to worry about their work, so they are less inclined to be ambitious about their work. Thus, 8% of the young people who attend one of the Free Churches say quite clearly that they are not interested in getting to the top of their work, compared with 4% of the Roman Catholics and 3% of the Anglicans.

The last two questions in this section look at the economic aspect of the young church-goers' attitude towards work. How important is it to them to have money to spend, and how important is their work in itself? While 94% of the young church-goers believe that it is important to them to work hard, only half of this number (45%) believe that spending money is important to them. The young church-goers attach a lot more importance to the intrinsic value of their work than to the money work can put into their pockets.

Most of the young church-goers seem to have been brought up to believe that work is important in its own right. Most of them say that they would rather be involved in a job they disliked than to live on Social Security income. Overall, just 14% of the young people say that they would rather go on Social Security than get a job they dislike doing. The girls (12%) are less likely than the boys (16%) to say that they would rather go on Social Security than get a job they do not like doing. The older teenagers (12%) are less likely to adopt this view than the younger teenagers (16%). While the churches may regard this kind of attitude towards work as laudable in an economic climate which can support full employment, in the serious situation of youth unemployment faced during the present decade, the churches need to be prepared to help their young members to accept being unemployed without blaming themselves for their predicament.

LEISURE

When they are not working, either in an educational sense or in an employment sense, how do these young church-goers fill their leisure time? How satisfied are they with their leisure activities? How does their church membership relate to the other spheres of leisure and recreational pursuits?

To begin with, the radio, television and music all play an important part in the leisure time of these young church-goers. For example, nine out of every ten (88%) of the young church-goers say that they often listen to music in their leisure time. The girls in particular find that music has an important part in their lives throughout the teenage years. 90% of the thirteen to fifteen year old girls and 91% of the sixteen to twenty year old girls often listen to music. The younger teenage boys are a little less inclined than the girls of the same age to listen to music, but in the later teenage years the interest shown by the boys matches that of the girls. Thus, 77% of the thirteen to fifteen year old boys and 90% of the sixteen to twenty year old boys often listen to music in their leisure time.

The teenage church-goers' interest in the radio and television is not simply limited to entertainment value. These young church-goers claim to take a keen interest in what is going on in the world and they do this by listening to the radio and television news broadcasts. Moreover, this interest in the radio and television news increases slightly with age. While the girls take a greater interest in music at a younger age than the boys, the boys find themselves taking a greater interest in the radio and television news at a younger age than the girls. Thus, 89% of the thirteen to fifteen year old boys and 92% of the sixteen to twenty year old boys say that they regularly listen to the radio or television news. 82% of the thirteen to fifteen year old girls and 91% of the sixteen to twenty year old girls regularly listen to the radio or television news.

The teenagers who attend church tend to be the kind of young people who enjoy reading. While less popular than radio and television, books find a regular place in the lives of nearly three quarters (72%) of the young church-goers. Although the proportion of the young church-goers who often read books is not significantly related to age, there are some interesting differences between the two sexes and between the three denominational groups.

The girls are much more likely to spend some of their leisure time reading than the boys. In fact, 79% of the girls say that they often read books in their leisure time, compared with 61% of the boys. The young Anglicans (78%) are more likely to read books in their leisure time than the young members of the Free Churches (73%), while the young members of the Free Churches are more likely to read books than the young Roman Catholics (67%).

Sport plays an important part in the lives of nearly two thirds of the young church-goers. Sport is more important to the younger teenagers than to the older teenagers. It is more important to the boys than to the girls. These trends remain consistent across the denominational groups. Almost exactly the same proportions of the young church-goers enjoy sport as a spectator pastime as enjoy it as a participant activity.

Looking first at sport as a participant activity, 79% of the thirteen to fifteen year old boys take an active part in sport, and this proportion falls by 10%, leaving 69% of the sixteen to twenty year old boys who also take an active part in sport. By way of comparison, 63% of the thirteen to fifteen year old girls take an active part in sport, and this falls to 55% among the sixteen to twenty year old girls. Looking next at sport as a spectator pastime, 77% of the thirteen to fifteen year old boys often watch sport in their leisure time, and this proportion falls by 7%, leaving 70% of the sixteen to twenty year old boys who often watch sport in their leisure time. By way of comparison, 64% of the thirteen to fifteen year old girls often watch sport in their leisure time, and this falls to 55% among the sixteen to twenty year olds.

A favoured recreation for a number of teenagers is to spend time in coffee bars or public houses with their friends. What proportion of the young church-goers consider that they spend a fair part of their leisure drinking with their friends? Because the thirteen to fifteen year olds are legally prohibited from drinking with their friends in public houses, we were asked by some of the churches to remove this question from the junior edition of the questionnaire. What we learn from the replies of the sixteen to twenty year olds is that three out of every seven (45%) of the church-goers in this age group often go drinking with their friends in their leisure time. This includes roughly the same proportion of the girls and the boys.

The teetotal tradition of some of the Free Churches is reflected, although not strongly, in the teenage church-goers' patterns of drinking behaviour. While 51% of the sixteen to twenty year old Roman Catholics and 46% of the Anglicans say that they often go drinking with their friends, only 35% of the sixteen to twenty year old members of the Free Churches participate in this leisure activity.

So far, we have looked in general terms at the proportions of the young church-goers who feel that they are the kind of people who like listening to music, watching television, reading, taking part in sport, going drinking with their friends, and so on. Another section of the questionnaire raised a set of more specific questions about the kind of leisure activities in which these young people had recently participated.

They were asked to tick against a list the leisure activities in which they had engaged within the previous three months.

Of the ten leisure-time activities listed in the questionnaire, the most popular overall were cinemas and discotheques. 56% of the young church-goers had been to the cinema within the past three months, and 55% had been to a discotheque. Next in order of priority were sports clubs, coffee bars and public houses. 42% of the young church-goers had been to a sports club within the past three months, 41% had been to coffee bars, and 38% had been to public houses. The other five listed activities lagged far behind. 18% had been to a non-church youth club, and 15% had belonged to one of the uniformed organisations, like the scouts or guides which was not church-sponsored. 9% had been to evening classes, 6% had been to bingo, and 3% had attended political meetings.

It is worth examining these ten activities in some detail in order to uncover the differences of the leisure preferences of the boys and the girls and the trends that occur according to age. The cinema and discotheque both gain in popularity with age. 63% of the sixteen to twenty year olds had been to the cinema within the past three months, compared with 49% of the thirteen to fifteen year olds. Similarly, 64% of the sixteen to twenty year olds had been to a discotheque, compared with 47% of the thirteen to fifteen year olds. Cinemas and discotheques are both more likely to attract the girls than the boys. 58% of the girls had been to the cinema within the past three months, compared with 52% of the boys. Similarly, 61% of the girls had been to a discotheque, compared with 47% of the boys.

Just as the girls were less likely to say that they were interested in sport, so they are less likely to have visited a sports club. 39% of the girls had been to a sports club within the past three months, compared with 47% of the boys. While interest in sport declines with age, the use of sports club facilities increases. After leaving school, the young people who wish to maintain an active part in sport need to join sports clubs and to use sports centres. Thus, 47% of the sixteen to twenty year olds have been to a sports centre within the past three months, compared with 37% of the thirteen to fifteen year olds.

Coffee bars were frequented within the past three months by a third (32%) of the thirteen to fifteen year olds and a half (51%) of the sixteen to twenty year olds. They were frequented by a third (34%) of the boys and by nearly a half (46%) of the girls. Although the thirteen to fifteen year olds are under the age for drinking in public houses, one in eight (12%) of this age group had in fact been to a pub within the past three months. This, however, is a leisure activity which rapidly increases with age, so that two thirds (68%) of the sixteen to twenty year olds had been to a pub within the past three months. While the girls are more likely to frequent the coffee bars, the pubs are frequented by an equal proportion of both sexes.

The popularity of the secular youth clubs and the non-church-sponsored uniformed organisations declines with age in exactly the same way as the popularity of the church youth clubs and church-sponsored uniformed organisations, which were discussed in chapter 3. While 21% of the thirteen to fifteen year olds had been to a secular youth club within the past three months, the proportion fell to 14% of the sixteen to twenty year olds. While 21% of the thirteen to fifteen year olds had been to a non-church-sponsored uniformed organisation like the scouts or guides within the past three months, the proportion fell to 9% of the sixteen to twenty year olds. The popularity of the secular youth club and the non-church-sponsored uniformed organisations is roughly the same among both sexes.

Evening classes and political meetings both attract more support from the older teenagers. 14% of the sixteen to twenty year olds had attended an evening class within the past three months, compared with 5% of the thirteen to fifteen year olds. 5% of the sixteen to twenty year olds had attended a political meeting within the past three months, compared with just 1% of the thirteen to fifteen year olds. Evening classes and political meetings attract an equal proportion of the boys and of the girls.

Finally, bingo attracts about one in twenty of the boys and girls from both age groups. Interest in bingo seems neither to increase nor to decrease among the teenage church-goers as they grow older.

The denominational allegiance of the young people is reflected in an interesting way in their preferences for leisure activities. This is seen most clearly in relationship to going to discotheques and drinking in public houses. The young members of the Free Churches are least likely to engage in these kinds of activities, while the young Roman Catholics are most likely to do so. For example, 60% of the sixteen to twenty year old members of the Free Churches visited a public house within the past three months, compared with 67% of the Anglicans and 71% of the Roman Catholics. 52% of the sixteen to twenty year old members of the Free Churches visited a discotheque within the past three months, compared with 66% of the Anglicans and 69% of the Roman Catholics.

As well as examining the popularity of the ten listed leisure time activities, the questionnaire also invited the young church-goers to describe any other activities in which they had engaged within the past three months. A very wide range of activities were instanced in response to this question. Some had been to concerts, rock festivals, folk clubs, or a music hall. Some had been to the theatre, or to the ballet. Some had been to music lessons, band practice, dancing classes. Some had been fishing, horse riding, dancing, sailing, swimming, roller-skating, ice-skating. Some had sung in choirs, played in orchestras or acted in a drama society. Some had been to parties, barbecues or out to restaurants or night clubs. Some had been to specialist activities, like a model railway society, an ornithological society or a chess club. Some had been to a football match, a greyhound stadium or a race course. Some had been to the young farmers' club, the young rotarians or to the St. John's Ambulance brigade. Some had practised orienteering, judo or karate. Some had been ten pin bowling, or to a fun fair. Some had been away on residential courses. Thus, in addition to their involvement with the local church, these teenage church-goers had also become involved in a wide range of other activities.

Having reviewed the ways in which these young people have spent their leisure time within the past three months, the final question concerns the extent to which they are satisfied with the use they make of their leisure time. Do they feel that they have enough to do, or are they bored for some of the time? Are they likely to be looking to the churches to fill more of their time, or are they so busy that they would refuse to take on anything more, however attractively arranged?

The clear request of half (51%) of the thirteen to fifteen year old church-goers is to have more things to do with their leisure time. Half of this age group feels that they are bored at least some of the time and would welcome some additional outlets for their energy and interests. Looked at from the other perspective, just 36% of the thirteen to fifteen year old girls and 42% of the thirteen to fifteen year old boys feel that their leisure time is totally and adequately occupied.

The situation looks somewhat different among the sixteen to twenty year olds. For many of the older teenagers the pressures of studying and of work have built up considerably. For many a wide range of social and recreational activities have opened up. While only 38% of the younger group were convinced that their leisure time was adequately occupied, 57% of the sixteen to twenty year olds find that their leisure time is fully occupied. While 51% of the younger group were actively looking for more things to do in their leisure time, only 36% of the sixteen to twenty year olds are in this position. If the churches have not already involved the thirteen to fifteen year olds in their activities, they will find it more difficult to recruit new sixteen to twenty year olds into these activities because the leisure time of the older age groups is generally more highly saturated.

Across the whole age range the young Roman Catholics are the most likely to be bored with their leisure time, while the young members of the Free Churches are the least likely to be bored. Thus, 47% of the young Roman Catholics said that they wished that they had more things to do with their leisure time, compared with 42% of the Anglicans and 37% of the teenagers who attend one of the Free Churches. These statistics need to be compared with the findings of chapter 3 which suggested that the young members of the Free Churches were most likely to be involved in weekday activities run by their church, either specially for young people or for adults as well, while the young Roman Catholics were least likely to be so involved.

10 WELL-BEING AND WORRY

The focus of the preceding six chapters has been on the beliefs and attitudes of the teenage church-goers over a wide range of issues. These chapters have reviewed the ways in which these young people think about the church, religion, moral issues, politics, social problems, their leisure time and their work. Now, the present chapter turns the attention inwards to examine what the young people are saying about themselves. Overall, how happy are they with their lives? What are their anxieties and worries? How much help do they feel that they need in coming to terms with life? Does belonging to a church help them at all?

In order to be systematic about this study of the personal lives and feelings of the young church-goers, the attitude inventory was designed to contain questions relating to four specific areas. This chapter will examine the young people's responses to each area in turn.

The first section examines the teenagers' overall response to life under the concept of *well-being*. What proportion of teenage church-goers feels that they enjoy a high level of psychological well-being? How many of them find their lives really worth living, at least most of the time? What kind of sense of purpose do they experience in life? What proportion of them lacks a true sense of psychological well-being? How many of them do not find their lives worth living and suffer from feelings of depression? Do any of them sometimes feel so fed up with life and with their inability to cope that they become troubled by suicidal thoughts and by the wish to escape from it all?

The second section reviews the amount of *worry* the young people experience as they grow up during the years of adolescence. How many of them are worried about their relationships, or about their sexuality? How many of them are worried about their physical or mental health? To what extent do the pressures of the teenage years make them feel unable to cope with life?

The third section examines the *self-concept* developed by the teenage church-goers. What do these young people think of themselves? How much importance do they attribute to their appearance and to their reputation? How important are friends to them, and how lonely do some of them become in the absence of friends? How outgoing are the young church attenders, or how introverted are they? How high a value do they place on their own worth?

The fourth section assesses the attitudes of the young church-goers to *counselling*. How many of them feel that they need to turn to other people for help and advice, and to whom are they most willing to turn? How helpful do they find their church when they need advice or counselling?

WELL-BEING

The term 'well-being' is used in social psychology as a way of talking about an individual's overall response to life. Those with a high level of well-being find life really worth living because they are well adjusted to their situation. Those with a low level of well-being find the tensions between themselves and their situations all too depressing and hopeless. Are the teenagers who are attracted to the churches the kind of young people who generally enjoy a high level of well-being, or do they tend to be unhappy and to experience frequent periods of depression? Are there any significant patterns in the levels of well-being displayed by the young people who attend different types of churches?

Their answers show that the majority of the young church-goers have a very positive response to life. Overall, they are not complaining about the way in which life treats them. Basically, they are content with the way in which things are going for them. 85% of the boys and 83% of the girls say that they find life really worth living. These proportions remain roughly stable across the age range.

To find life worth living is one thing; to feel that life really has a sense of purpose and is actually going somewhere is another thing. Significantly fewer of the young church-goers are convinced of their purpose in life than are convinced of their enjoyment of life. While 83% of the thirteen to fifteen year olds are confident that they find life really worth living, the proportion falls to 62% who feel that their life has a sense of purpose. However, the feeling of a sense of purpose in life is something which grows stronger during the next few years, so that 73% of the sixteen to twenty year olds share this conviction. These proportions remain roughly stable across both sexes.

The other side of well-being is depression and despair. While the churches were content to allow the younger teenagers to be asked questions about their happiness, some of the churches thought it inappropriate that young people should be faced with questions about their negative responses to life. Depression, despair and feelings of alienation from life were matters from which the churches thought it appropriate to protect the younger teenagers. Consequently, in examining the other side of well-being, the data are restricted to the sixteen to twenty year olds.

Although the majority of the sixteen to twenty year olds say that they find their lives really worth living, this does not mean that none of them knows the darker side of life and that none of them experiences very real periods of gloom and despair. In fact, one in three (32%) of the sixteen to twenty year olds say that they often experience periods of depression.

Fits of depression and mood-swings are a part of the facts of life for the adolescent years, during the period of transition from childhood to adulthood. The present data demonstrate that the young people who attend church are no exception to the general rule. In accordance with the general pattern revealed by other research projects, the girls (34%) are more likely to experience frequent periods of depression than the boys (28%).

The most severe moods of depression are those which breed suicidal thoughts. Do young church-goers ever sink so far into the depths of depression that they have considered taking their own lives? Almost half of those who admit to experiencing frequent periods of depression also admit to having sometimes considered taking their own lives. In more precise terms, this means that 13% of the sixteen to twenty year old church-going boys and 17% of the sixteen to twenty year old church-going girls confessed to having entertained suicidal thoughts.

In contemplating the information given in the preceding paragraph it is essential to grasp that we are talking about suicidal feelings and not about suicidal activity. Very few of the young people who say that they have entertained suicidal thoughts and feelings are likely to have gone as far as initiating a suicide attempt. However, this is no reason for taking their words less than seriously. Not only does the presence of suicidal thoughts indicate a deep level of despair and unhappiness with life, it also draws attention to a whole area of potential risk should these thoughts predominate and should the seeds of despair which they represent find a good soil in which to germinate.

Behind these statistics there are some important denominational differences. Because not all the questions in this section were posed to the younger age group, these denominational differences are most clearly seen among the sixteen to twenty year olds. What we learnt from this older age group is that the young Roman Catholics feel that they enjoy a lower level of well-being than the young Anglicans and the young members of the Free Churches.

To begin with, 82% of the sixteen to twenty year old Roman Catholics say that they find life really worth living, compared with 88% of the Anglicans and 90% of the Free Church members. A similar trend is revealed by the fact that 69% of the sixteen to twenty year old Roman Catholics feel that their lives have a sense of purpose, compared with 77% of the Anglicans and 77% of the Free Church members. It is totally consistent with this trend that the young Roman Catholics are slightly more likely to say that often feel depressed (34%) than the young Anglicans (30%) or the young members of the Free Churches (30%). The young Roman Catholics are also slightly more likely to report suicidal thoughts (18%) than the young Anglicans (14%) or the young members of the Free Churches (14%).

In being alert to the pastoral needs of their sixteen to twenty year old members, the churches would be wise to take fully into account the fact that one in three of them knows what it is to experience frequent moods of depression, and that one in six of them sometimes entertains suicidal thoughts.

WORRY

The adolescent years are a time of considerable self-doubt and anxiety. Accelerated growth and bodily changes impose a range of strains on the adolescent boy and girl. The discovery of a new personal identity and developing awareness of sexuality place friendships and relationships in a new light. The adolescent years are a time of new situations and fresh discoveries. How well are the teenage church-goers coping with all this or how likely are they to feel themselves to be under pressure and worried by it all?

One in three of the young people feels that relationships are a particular cause of anxiety to him or her. The girls are a little more likely than the boys to feel that relationships are difficult to cope with. Thus, 31% of the boys and 36% of the girls report that they are worried about their relationships with other people. This is equally true for the young people from the Free Churches, the Roman Catholic Church and the Anglican Church.

The proportion of young people who remain actively worried about their relationships remains constant over the age period from thirteen to twenty years. At the same time, the number of those who are positively confident about their relationships increases slightly from 42% among the thirteen to fifteen year olds to 48% among the sixteen to twenty year olds. This means that, while 25% of the thirteen to fifteen year olds are still trying to work out whether they are succeeding in their relationships or not, this proportion falls to 17% of the sixteen to twenty year olds.

An important aspect of the making and breaking of relationships during the teenage years concerns the exploration and testing of aspects of developing sexuality. Sex, however, was another of those words which some of the churches wished to shield from the younger teenagers. So, once again, we have no idea from the survey how the thirteen to fifteen year olds were feeling about their developing sexual identity. This is unfortunate, since these years may be some of the most important and formative in shaping the young person's responses and attitudes.

Three out of four (74%) of the sixteen to twenty year old church-goers feel that they have no problems about their sex lives. The remaining one in four is not so sure. 11% of the sixteen to twenty year old boys and 8% of the sixteen to twenty year old girls say that they are really worried about their sex lives. Another 16% of the boys and another 18% of the girls feel that they are worried from time to time about their sex lives, although they are not really sure just how deeply that worry goes.

The sixteen to twenty year olds who attend one of the Free Churches are more likely to say that they are not worried about their sex lives (85%) than either the Roman Catholics (73%) or the Anglicans (70%). This could reflect the fact that the young Free Church members are more likely to be well adjusted to their sexuality, or that they are more likely to be reticent about discussing sexual problems.

While relationships are a cause of anxiety to a third of the young teenagers, their health is a cause of anxiety to a quarter of them. Again, the young girls are more likely than the boys to feel that their physical health presents a problem to them. Thus, 27% of the thirteen to fifteen year old girls and 22% of the thirteen to fifteen year old boys report that they are worried about their health. Looked at from the other perspective, their physical health is seen as clearly not being a cause of anxiety by 65% of the boys and 56% of the girls.

Their physical health continues to become less of a source of anxiety as they grow into the later teenage years. Among the sixteen to twenty year olds the proportion of boys who are worried about their health falls from 22% to 15%. The proportion of girls who are worried about their health falls from 27% also to 15%.

The denominational difference is again significant, with the young members of the Free Churches exhibiting less anxiety about their physical health than the young members from the other churches. Over the whole age range, only 10% of the Free Church members report that they are worried about their health, compared with 21% of the Anglicans and 21% of the Roman Catholics.

To what extent do the pressures of life in the adolescent years cause the teenage church-goers to be anxious about their ability to cope with life? As many as one in five (21%) of the thirteen to fifteen year olds are in fact worried that they cannot cope. The young teenage girls (25%) are more likely to suffer from this anxiety than the young teenage boys (17%). Looked at from the other perspective, among the thirteen to fifteen year olds, 61% of the boys and 48% of the girls are confident about their ability to cope.

The confidence of the young church-goers in their ability to cope with life continues to grow into the later teenage years. Among the sixteen to twenty year olds, the proportion of girls who are worried about their ability to cope falls from 25% to 18%; the proportion of boys who are worried about their ability to cope falls from 17% to 12%.

Just as the young members of the Free Churches exhibit less anxiety about their physical health than the other young church-goers, so they are less likely to record anxiety about their ability to cope. Over the whole age range, 14% of the Free Church members say that they are worried that they cannot cope, compared with 18% of the Anglicans and 21% of the Roman Catholics.

The anxiety that one is unable to cope with life can lead, in its most severe form, to the fear that one will head towards a nervous breakdown. Are any of the young people who attend church likely to be questioning their ability to cope with life as seriously as all this? This is another of those questions which some of the churches thought it inappropriate to address to the younger teenagers. The replies of the older teenagers indicate that 5% of the boys and 7% of the girls are in fact worried that they might have a breakdown.

This kind of anxiety affects roughly the same proportions of the young people from the Anglican, Roman Catholic and Free Churches. In other words, one out of every sixteen or seventeen sixteen to twenty year olds who come into contact with the churches may need the kind of pastoral help which will enable them to deal with the very radical questioning of their ability to cope with life.

SELF CONCEPT

Like well-being, 'self concept' is another of those terms used by psychologists with a variety of meanings. In this chapter, I am using the term self concept quite differently from the way in which I used the related term 'self image' in my earlier studies of sixteen to twenty-five year olds and of twenty-six to thirty-nine year olds. I used the term self image to discuss the way in which people attempt to project themselves to others. I am now using the term self concept to discuss the way in which they understand their own basic personal values. The teenage years are a time during which the young person develops a growing awareness of his or her identity as an individual. All the social and peer group pressures emphasise that is it important for this identity to be acceptable within the prevailing norms of teenage culture. One of the signs of this process of growing awareness is the way in which the teenagers take an increasing interest in their appearance. So, then, just how much importance do the young church-goers place on their appearance?

The girls are more conscious of their appearance from a younger age than are the boys. Among the thirteen to fifteen year olds, 91% of the girls are already very committed to the idea that their appearance is important to them, and this level remains constant throughout the rest of the teenage years. The importance of their appearance is directly denied by only four in every hundred thirteen to fifteen year old girls and by just two in every hundred sixteen to twenty year old girls.

The thirteen to fifteen year old boys are less conscious of their appearance than the girls of the same age. Nevertheless, three out of four (75%) of the thirteen to fifteen year old boys are saying that their appearance is important to them. The proportion increases to 85% of the sixteen to twenty year old boys. The importance of their appearance is directly denied by twelve in every hundred of the thirteen to fifteen year old boys and by ten in every hundred of the sixteen to twenty year old boys.

There are no denominational differences among the younger teenagers in relationship to the importance they attach to their appearance. However, among the sixteen to twenty year olds, a very significant difference does emerge. The sixteen to twenty year olds who belong to the Free Churches (77%) are less likely to regard their appearance as important than those who belong to either the Roman Catholic (90%) or Anglican (93%) churches.

Next to appearance comes the idea of reputation. Not only are teenagers concerned about what they look like, they are also concerned about what other people think about them. Just as the girls are more concerned about their appearance than the boys, so they are also more concerned about their reputation. This time, however, there are no significant differences between the two age groups or between the various denominational groups. Throughout the sample, 69% of the boys and 78% of the girls say that what people think of them is important to them.

Teenagers are highly gregarious. Generally they like to be able to mix with other people of their own age and they place a high premium on friendship. Teenagers are extremely aware of the important part played by friends during this period of growing self awareness. Less than one teenager in a hundred denies the importance of friends in his or her life.

The importance which young church-goers place on their appearance, their reputation and their friendships, has far reaching implications for the churches themselves. It is all too easy for adult worshippers to show disapproval of a young person's appearance, to make it known that they dislike the way the young dress or wear their hair. Disapproval and criticism of this kind is a sure way to alienate the young church-goer. At the same time, the importance of friendships in the teenager's life often means that one alienated young person leads to the alienation of the whole group. Similarly, a group of young friends who find themselves accepted within the worshipping community may well retain their loyalty to the church more securely than the isolated one or two teenagers who look for all their peer group support outside the worshipping community.

The fact that they are so aware of their need for friends also means that those whose need for friends is not fully met can become acutely and painfully aware of their loneliness. Churches probably think of themselves as social places through which friendships can be formed and sustained. At the same time, they need to be sensitive to the proportion of their young members who are in fact conscious of their loneliness. Overall, one in six of the teenagers who attend church describe themselves as lonely people.

Young male and young female church attenders have an equal likelihood of being lonely. For both boys and girls this likelihood increases with age. Thus 21% of the sixteen to twenty year olds say that they tend to be lonely people, compared with 14% of the thirteen to fifteen year olds. While there are no significant denominational differences among the younger teenagers, among the sixteen to twenty year olds the Roman Catholics (25%) are more likely to be lonely young people than the Anglicans (19%) or the members of the Free Churches (17%).

In its more extreme form, loneliness can be very isolating. About ten in every hundred of the young church-goers feel so lonely that it seems to them that no-one really knows them. These young people have not built up the sort of relationships which allow them the experiences of trust and confidence to share their true identity. The feeling that no-one really knows them is experienced more by the sixteen to twenty year olds (13%) than by the thirteen to fifteen year olds (8%). It is experienced more by the girls (13%) than by the boys (7%). Again, among the older age group, it tends to be experienced more among the young Roman Catholics (15%) than among the young members of the Free Churches (9%), with the young Anglicans occupying a middle position (12%).

Other research studies which I have undertaken have demonstrated that the young people who are interested in religion tend to be slightly more introverted than those who do not take an interest in religion. Introverts are more withdrawn, more shy, less out-going and less sociable than extraverts. This, of course, does not mean that all teenage church-goers are the sort of people who try to escape from the crowd into their own corner. Well over half of the young people in the sample feel happy in the crowd and say that they like to have a lot of people around them. In fact the girls who attend church (59%) are more likely to feel this way than the boys (49%). There are no major age or denominational trends in this pattern.

On the other hand, there is a number of young church-goers (23%) who report that they do find crowds oppressive. These young people are evenly distributed over the age group, between the two sexes and across the different denominations. The churches need to be sensitive to the way in which these more introverted young church-goers tend to respond negatively to large crowds and some group activities. It is important that the socially-orientated congregation should not frighten these young people away.

Another sign of introversion is the desire to play safe, to think before leaping and to avoid situations, places and people who may threaten or frighten. What proportion of the teenage church-goers think of themselves as being in this kind of category? One in five (19%) of the thirteen to fifteen year olds feel that they try to avoid things that are a little frightening and this proportion increases to one in four (24%) of the sixteen to twenty year olds. The girls (26%) recognise themselves as being more introverted in this way than the boys (15%). This is important information to keep in mind when planning certain activities and certain situtations for young church-goers.

Before leaving this section on self concept, we turn attention to the value which the young church-goers place on themselves. Some people argue that an implication of the Christian gospel concerns the discovery of one's own value or worth in the eyes of God. Others might emphasise an alternative interpretation according to which the individual discovers his or her own worthlessness in comparison with God's holiness and grace. In the light of these conflicting theologies, it becomes important to look closely at precisely what the young church-goers are saying about their own values or worth, and to examine whether there are in fact any denominational differences on this issue.

What the attitude inventory particularly wanted to monitor was the proportion of the young teenagers who adopt a self-effacing and self-deprecatory attitude towards themselves. Once again, some of the participating churches thought this to be an inappropriate area of enquiry for the younger teenagers, leaving us with information relating to the older group only. The conclusion is that one in nine (12%) of the sixteen to twenty year old church-goers reports that he or she does not feel that he or she is worth much as a person. This proportion is basically constant for both sexes across the various denominational groups. While the majority of the teenage church-goers appears to have a positive self concept, the churches need to be sensitive to the situation of the minority who think more negatively of themselves.

COUNSELLING

Having discovered the proportions of the young church-goers who admit to being worried, lonely, depressed and even suicidal, we turn next to examine the way in which they perceive their needs to turn to other people for help and for advice. How many of them long for help and advice, and to whom do they turn? How many of them turn to the church for help, and what do think of the way in which the church has responded to them?

At the time of completing the questionnaire, nearly one in three (31%) of the teenage church-goers felt that they often longed for someone to turn to for advice. This represents a very substantial pastoral need. The question which the churches have to face concerns the extent to which their pastoral concern for their young members is able to respond to such a need. It is, of course, important to whom young people turn for advice. The kind of advice they receive depends upon the kind of people to whom they turn. Ideally, young church-goers should feel able to turn to people within their churches, but often this is impeded by lack of time and by lack of trust.

The proportion of the young church-goers who long for someone to turn to for advice remains constant over the teenage years. The sixteen to twenty year olds feel neither a greater nor a lesser need to turn to others for advice than the thirteen to fifteen year olds. Throughout the age range, the girls (34%) are a little more likely to long to turn to someone for advice than the boys (27%). The young Roman Catholics (33%) are more likely to long for someone to whom to turn for advice than the young members of the Free Churches (26%), with the young Anglicans occupying a midway position (29%).

The first person to whom the younger teenagers turn for advice is their mother. Overall, two thirds (67%) of the thirteen to fifteen year olds say that they find it helpful to talk about their problems with their mother. At this age, the girls are considerably closer to their mother than the boys. 74% of the thirteen to fifteen year old girls say that they find it helpful to talk about their problems with their mother, compared with 57% of the boys. As the girls grow older, however, they tend to feel less close to their mothers and to be less able to discuss personal problems with them. Thus among the sixteen to twenty year old girls, the proportion who feel that it is helpful to talk about their problems with their mother drops from 74% to 66%. The proportion of the boys who feel that it is helpful to talk about their problems with their mother remains stable over the teenage years.

Teenagers are much less likely to feel that they are able to talk about their problems with their father than with their mother. While two thirds (67%) of the thirteen to fifteen year olds find it helpful to talk about their problems with their mother, well under one third (28%) of this age group feel that it is helpful to talk with their father.

Moreover, the proportion of the young church-goers who feel that it is helpful to talk with their fathers does not increase with age. Just as 28% of the thirteen to fifteen year olds find their fathers helpful people to whom they can talk, so only 29% of the sixteen to twenty year olds find this to be the case. While the girls feel closer to their mothers than the boys, the reverse is not the case when it comes to their relationships with their fathers. The boys are not significantly more likely than the girls to find it helpful to talk about their problems with their father.

The amount of support which the young church-goers feel they derive from talking their problems through with their parents differs significantly between the denominations. The young Anglicans feel that they are better supported by their parents than either the young Roman Catholics or the young members of the Free Churches. 69% of the young Anglicans say that they find it helpful to talk about their problems with their mother, compared with 62% of the Roman Catholics and 59% of the Free Church members. Similarly, 33% of the young Anglicans say that they find it helpful to talk about their problems with their father, compared with 28% of the Free Church members and 26% of the Roman Catholics.

While mother is the first person to whom the younger teenagers turn for advice, the older teenagers tend to place their close friends in first position. Three quarters (74%) of the sixteen to twenty year olds say that they find it helpful to talk about their problems with close friends, compared with 61% of this age group who find it helpful to talk with their mother and 29% who find it helpful to talk with their father.

The girls are much more likely than the boys to develop the kind of close friendship through which they talk out their personal problems, and they do so from an earlier age. Thus, among the thirteen to fifteen year olds, already 73% of the girls are experiencing the help which comes from talking over their problems with close friends, compared with 39% of the boys. Among the sixteen to twenty year olds, the proportion of girls who share this experience increases from 73% to 84%, while the proportion of the boys increases from 39% to 59%.

Just as in the earlier section, the older Roman Catholics emerged as significantly more lonely than their contemporaries who attend the other churches, so now they emerge as being less likely to have the kind of friends with whom they can discuss their personal problems. Only 69% of the sixteen to twenty year old Roman Catholics report that they find it helpful to talk about their problems with close friends, compared with 79% of the Anglicans and 78% of the Free Church members of the same age.

Parents and friends are, understandably, much more accessible to the teenagers who want to discuss their problems than the minister of their church. Indeed, it is not unusual for the teenagers to find it difficult to engage the sympathy and understanding of the clergy, while the clergy find it equally difficult to appreciate the immediacy and urgency of the problems which confront the teenagers who attend church. Consequently, there is only a comparatively small proportion (14%) of the thirteen to fifteen year olds who report that they have found it helpful to discuss their problems with a minister of religion. While the proportion of the young church-goers who have been helped by their clergy increases significantly among the sixteen to twenty year olds, still only one in five (22%) of this age group have established this kind of relationship with their clergy.

Among the younger teenagers, there is no significant difference in the proportions of the boys and of the girls who have found it helpful to talk about their problems with a minister of religion. Among the older teenagers, the girls are more likely than the boys to have turned to the clergy and to have been helped by them. Thus, among the sixteen to twenty year olds, the proportion of the girls helped by the clergy increases from 14% to 25%, while the proportion of the boys increases less sharply from 14% to 18%.

There is also an important denominational difference in the proportions of the sixteen to twenty year olds who have found it helpful to talk about their problems with a minister of religion. The sixteen to twenty year olds who attend one of the Free Churches (36%) are much more likely to have experienced help from their minister than those who attend the Roman Catholic (18%) or Anglican (19%) churches. The Free Church clergy seem to have succeeded in developing a closer pastoral relationship with their older teenage members than the Anglican or Roman Catholic clergy.

Seeing that only a comparatively small proportion of the teenagers who attend church have successfully turned to the clergy for advice, it is important to look more closely at their image of the clergy as counsellors. If they had the opportunity to talk their problems over with the clergy, would the teenage church-goers take the opportunity, or would they be distrustful of doing so?

The answer is that the majority of the thirteen to fifteen year olds who attend church remain unconvinced of the approachability of the clergy and of their acceptability as counsellors. In fact, only one in four (26%) of the young church-goers in this age group are confident that they would turn to the clergy to discuss their problems should the need and opportunity arise. A larger proportion of them, one in three (34%), are firmly convinced that they would never discuss their problems with the clergy. The remaining 40% waver in a situation of indecision, not being sure whether they would want to turn to the clergy or not.

The sixteen to twenty year old church-goers have a more positive attitude towards the clergy as counsellors than the younger teenagers. Nevertheless, only three out of seven (44%) of the sixteen to twenty year old church-goers are convinced that they would talk over their problems with a minister of religion, while 27% remain adamant that they would never discuss their problems with the clergy. The remaining

29% have not closed off the possibility of turning to the clergy, although they remain far from sure of their willingness to do so.

Again, the denominational differences among the sixteen to twenty year olds are very interesting. The Roman Catholics are the most likely to reject the possibility of discussing their problems with a clergyman, while the Free Church members are least likely to reject this possibility. Thus, 33% of the sixteen to twenty year old Roman Catholics say that they would never discuss their problems with the clergy, compared with 25% of the Anglicans and only 12% of the members of the Free Churches. It would seem, then, that the young Roman Catholics' training in confessing their sins before the clergy discourages them from seeing the clergy as counsellors rather than encouraging them to trust the clergy as counsellors.

11 CHARACTER SKETCHES

The purpose of the preceding chapters has been to make generalisations about teenage church-goers as a group. These chapters set out to compare the responses of boys and girls, to discuss how their responses change as they grow older, and to examine how much the denominational groups differ from each other. This kind of analysis has had a central part to play in our attempt to understand the relationship between teenagers and the church today. However, this kind of analysis is only part of the story.

As well as leading to statistical generalisations, the information collected by the attitude inventory enables us to draw up detailed character sketches for each of the individual teenagers who co-operated in the project. Space would never permit thirteen hundred detailed character studies, but a few such studies can usefully serve to illustrate the richness of the data and remind us that, beneath the useful generalisations, we are the whole time dealing with uniqueness and individuality. In the last analysis, one of the greatest benefits of sociological generalisations about young people is the way in which these generalisations help us to gain insight into the individuals whom we know and among whom we work.

The five character studies presented in this chapter are not claimed to be representative of teenage church-goers in any sense. There is possibly no such thing as a typical teenage church-goer. The few young people chosen for in-depth study were chosen virtually at random from the total batch of the questionnaires included in the study: Elizabeth is a fourteen year old Anglican; Martin is a fifteen year old Baptist; Carole is seventeen years old and worships at a new ecumenical centre; David is a nineteen year old Anglican; Mary is an eighteen year old Roman Catholic. The names attributed to these five young people are pseudonyms. Moreover, there is no way in which the completed questionnaires can be traced back to the individuals who completed them. The five character studies are based on real people, but the anonymity of these people is completely preserved.

ELIZABETH

Elizabeth is a fourteen year old Anglican from the city of Lancaster. Her parents first sent her to Sunday school when she was four, and she has been regularly attending church services since the age of seven. When she was eight she joined the church-sponsored brownie pack associated with her church. When she was old enough, she graduated from the brownies into the church-sponsored guides. Just last year, she joined the church youth club for teenagers.

Going to church on a Sunday morning is very much part of Elizabeth's weekly routine. She attends just one service each Sunday, but she rarely misses this service. She prefers to go to the mid-morning family service, which does not include the celebration of holy communion. This is a well attended service which attracts a number of young people. Elizabeth reckons that there were more than fifty teenagers in the congregation last week.

Elizabeth comes from a professional home background. Her father is a lecturer in engineering at a college, and her mother works as a secretary. Although her parents sent Elizabeth to an Anglican Sunday school from an early age, they are not active members of the church themselves. Elizabeth has now grown through the Sunday school to become a regular member of the congregation, but she finds that she is the only person in her household who regularly goes to Sunday services. For this reason, she has to go to church alone.

Elizabeth has not yet been confirmed, but she is currently a member of the confirmation class in her church, and she looks forward to being confirmed in the near future. Her church believes in a thorough programme of preparation for confirmation; Elizabeth has already belonged to the confirmation class for nearly a year.

The weekly confirmation class, the weekly church youth club, and the weekly meeting of the church-sponsored guide group keep Elizabeth in very close contact with her church. She also occasionally attends a weekday church service. On the other hand, Elizabeth has no contact with any church-based discussion groups, prayer groups or study groups, arranged either specifically for young people or for people of all ages.

However, the church youth club provides a certain number of opportunities for Elizabeth to join in discussion over a wide range of issues. The two topics most frequently raised at the youth club are the bible and current pop music. The next two topics most frequently raised are prayer and television. Less frequently, the group has talked about personal relationships and the environment. The youth club leaders, thus, seem to try to approach issues from both the explicitly Christian direction and from the members' own experience. On the other hand, there are a number of issues which have not been raised at the youth club which Elizabeth would value the chance to discuss. These include politics, marriage, work and the occult. She is not interested in widening the discussion to include issues like the Third World, racism, unemployment, law and order, and cults like the moonies.

Although Elizabeth has been attending the same church for a number of years, she has never become involved in taking an active part in the services, apart from one or two occasions when she has been invited to play a musical instrument. Her failure to take an active part in the services has been because of the lack of opportunity, rather than of the lack of interest or willingness. She says that no one has ever asked her to become more involved. If given the invitation, Elizabeth would like to become involved as an altar server and as a bell ringer. She would value the opportunity to assist as a sidesperson, giving out books and serving refreshments. She would like the chance to make a contribution to worship through leading singing, and by taking a part in liturgical dance or drama. On the other hand, she does not feel that she wants to take a part in conducting the worship itself, in leading prayers, reading lessons or preaching the sermon. She is not interested in taking the collection, one of the jobs more frequently offered to young people in church services.

As yet, Elizabeth has not been offered any positions of responsibility in her church. She feels that matters like serving on the church council and deanery synod are rightly left to older people, and she has no desire to undertake such responsibilities as yet. However, she feels that she could be making a more responsible contribution to the life of her church than she is currently given the opportunity to do. For example, she feels that she might be able to offer something useful as a Sunday school teacher, or as the leader of a children's group. She would also like to serve on a committee responsible for the church youth club to which she belongs.

Looking to the future, Elizabeth feels that there are quite a number of things which should be given a higher priority in the life of her local church, and she says that she would be willing to become involved in some of them herself. For example, she says that she would be willing to give more time to church groups concerned with learning what it means to be a Christian, or learning more about prayer and worship. She feels that the church should be more involved in the neighbourhood, both conducting evangelism and helping people who are in need. She feels that the church should give more time to exploring ecumenical projects at the local level, and to becoming more involved in the church's missionary work overseas. She would value the opportunity to become involved in church groups through which she could share her thoughts, feelings and problems. What she is not interested in her church doing is giving more time to the problems of the Third World, or to campaigning on local issues. Elizabeth's vision of the church is not that of a political church.

Although Elizabeth continues to attend her church regularly, she finds herself becoming more and more impatient with the life of that church. She feels that the Sunday services she attends are old-fashioned, extremely boring, lifeless and out of touch with young people today. She cannot imagine any of her friends who do not usually go to church being able to turn up to one of these services and getting anything out of the experience at all.

Elizabeth blames both the vicar and the older people who attend her church for the church's failure to appeal to young people today. She feels that the vicar of her church is very old-fashioned and out of touch with life today. He comes over to young people as someone who is rather aloof and who has nothing to say to them. Elizabeth feels that he does not get on well with children or teenagers. He fails to listen to them and does not understand what they are trying to say. His sermons are boring and irrelevant to their daily lives.

Elizabeth feels that the older people in her church are a very unfriendly bunch. They appear unfriendly to each other, and even more so to the young people who attend the church. Elizabeth believes that the young people who attend church really want to see some changes take place in the services, but these young people are totally unable to influence church policy. The older people refuse to accept change, and their views win the day. In fact, the older members of the congregation do their best to keep the younger members from having any say in church policy. Elizabeth reckons that, if the younger church-goers could have their way, their church would make much more use of modern music, modern hymns, and modern forms of service.

Elizabeth feels that the attitude of the older church members is a particular shame because the church has quite a large teenage membership. These teenagers she believes to be a friendly group of young people. They mix well with their peers who do not attend church. If the older people were more friendly and more willing to except change, Elizabeth reckons that her church would be able to open its doors to many more teenagers like herself.

At the end of her questionnaire, commenting on her local church, Elizabeth wrote, 'my church could offer more by making the church look modern and really let people join in instead of being spectators. My church seems to lose young people after they have been confirmed. I believe it is because they are old-fashioned. The church should become modern. My church hasn't helped me much. I found I believed more strongly when I went to my friend's church. They are friendly to strangers. When I am confirmed I will go there.'

In spite of her negative attitude towards her local church, Elizabeth feels very sure of the reality of God and of the part played by God in her own life. She is convinced that God has guided her life, and she is able to look back with confidence to a particular turning point in her life when she accepted Christ as her personal saviour. There have been times when she has been particularly conscious of the presence and of the power of God within her. She says that she knows what it is to speak of a religious experience.

Elizabeth says that her religion is very important to her. She has no doubts about her belief in God or in the teachings of the church. She believes firmly in the resurrection of Jesus and in the doctrine that Jesus Christ is the Son of God. She believes firmly in the doctrine of life after death, although she continues to hold alongside this some belief in reincarnation. In some ways, Elizabeth's beliefs are quite fundamentalist. She accepts literally the Genesis tradition that God made the world in six days and then rested on the seventh. Elizabeth is convinced that religious education has an important part to play in schools.

Because the reality of God is important in Elizabeth's life, she says that she tries to take the responsibility and discipline of prayer seriously. She sets aside some time every day for private prayer. On the other hand, she takes bible reading much less seriously and only occasionally reads the bible by herself. She never thinks of saying a grace before meals.

Although she has been a regular worshipper in an Anglican church since the age of seven, Elizabeth has also found the opportunity to worship with other Christian denominations. She has attended services in Baptist, Methodist, United Reformed Church and Roman Catholic churches. On the other hand, Elizabeth has had no personal experience of any of the other major world faiths or of any other religious groups. She is ecumenically minded but equally emphatic that Christianity is the only true religion.

Elizabeth is a very honest young person of considerable integrity. She says that she always tries to own up when she makes a mistake. She is open and honest about the fact that she has sometimes broken her promise or told a lie. She admits that she has sometimes taken advantage of people. She owns up to the fact that she sometimes feels resentful when she does not get her own way and that she has been jealous when others seem to get on better than she does. She cannot honestly claim that she has never taken anything which did not belong to her.

Elizabeth believes that the law needs to be obeyed, even when she is unsure of the reasons behind the law. She argues that it is wrong to sell cigarettes to children under the legal age. She believes that motoring laws should be strictly upheld, however inconvenient they may be. She is totally unwilling to condone travelling on public transport without a ticket.

Elizabeth argues that moral values are extremely important to her. Unfortunately, we are unable to examine her specific moral attitudes in depth, because she completed the shorter form of the attitude inventory. Her views on contraception, sex outside marriage, homosexuality and pornography remain unknown to us. What we do know is that she is concerned that divorce is becoming too easy to obtain in today's society. Similarly, we do not know her views about abortion, but we do know that she is willing to support the idea of euthanasia. While her views on drugs are also unknown, we know that she strongly disapproves of the abuse of alcohol.

Although she is not very well informed about politics, Elizabeth enthusiastically follows her parents' support for the Conservative party. She does not know what to make of the Liberal party. She dismisses the Labour party out of hand. She claims to place all her political confidence in the Conservative party. However, she remains very vague about her views on specific political issues. For example, she is critical of the trade unions, but has no ideas about the pros or cons of the nationalisation of industry.

The work of the National Front has come to Elizabeth's attention, and she says that she is very strongly opposed to that movement. She is, however, far from sure how she personally feels about the presence of ethnic minorities in her own area. She remains convinced that immigration restrictions should be enforced.

Elizabeth takes very little interest in the wider issues of world politics. She professes to have no views on global matters like the threat of nuclear war or the risks of pollution to the environment. Nearer to home, she is left untouched by the problems of inflation and unemployment. She does not feel that these issues impinge directly on her personal life and, for this reason, she believes that she can ignore them.

Elizabeth is aware of the poverty of the Third World and of the problems of homelessness, but again she feels that these issues are too removed from her immediate environment to be of real concern to her. After all, she says, there is nothing that she can do to solve the world's problems.

At the age of fourteen, Elizabeth is, naturally, still at school. She is attending a local Church of England voluntary aided secondary school, where she is studying a mixture of arts and science subjects. She is very happy at this school and she likes her class-mates very much. She is ambitious and is prepared to work hard at school. She often worries about her school work, but is not unhappy about it.

Quite often, Elizabeth finds that she is bored with her leisure time. In spite of her regular commitment to the church youth club, guides and the confirmation class, Elizabeth often wishes that she had more things to do with her leisure time. Within the past three months, she has been to the cinema, to discotheques, and to the local coffee bar. At home she spends a lot of her time reading books. She also watches some television, although she says that she generally prefers reading to watching television. Sport plays almost no part in her life. She has no interest in watching sport, and even less interest in taking part in sport.

Generally speaking, Elizabeth says that she is very happy with her life. She finds life really worth living, and she feels that her life has a genuine sense of purpose. She has a number of friends and enjoys their company a great deal. She is an outgoing sort of person. She likes having a lot of people around her and she finds it important to be popular. It matters to her a great deal what her friends think about her, and she takes considerable trouble to create a good impression among them.

Underneath it all, however, Elizabeth is by no means as secure as she would like other people to think. She often worries about her school work and about her ability to cope with life. Sometimes she becomes anxious about her health and about her relationships. Sometimes she feels acutely lonely and needs someone with whom to talk. Fortunately, she has a close relationship with her mother and is able to turn to her mother when she needs help or advice. Her relationship with her father is much more difficult and she tries never to talk with him about things that really matter to her. Elizabeth has never felt confident enough in her vicar to want to turn to him for advice or counselling, and she cannot imagine ever wanting to do so in the future.

Elizabeth is a teenager who has stuck with her local church for a great number of years, without much by way of parental support or encouragement. She is now a well-established member of the confirmation class. Her vicar may well be content that she is on the way to becoming a fully committed member of his church. Elizabeth, however, has already made up her mind that this church has nothing to offer her, and that she will seek to attach herself to another congregation as soon as she has been confirmed. If her experience in the next congregation is no less promising than her present experience, Elizabeth may well soon be joining those large ranks of confirmed, but non-practising Anglicans.

MARTIN

Martin is a fifteen year old member of the Baptist Church. He has been attending church services regularly with his parents since the age of five. He says that he was admitted into adult membership of the Baptist Church when he was eleven years of age. He had been prepared for admission to adult membership by a course of instruction lasting about six months.

Martin's father is the headmaster of a primary school and his mother the school secretary at another school. Martin attends the local county secondary school where he specialises in science subjects.

Last Sunday Martin went along to the mid-morning communion service at the Baptist chapel with his mother and father. There were a dozen or so other teenagers attending this service as well. Martin does not go to services every Sunday. He reckons to attend services on average every other Sunday, but he also attends the occasional mid-week service.

Apart from his fortnightly attendance at service, Martin's contact with his church is really rather weak. He has never belonged to any form of Sunday school, church children's group or church youth group. Within the past three months he has attended no church meetings arranged either specifically for teenagers or for people of all ages. He has joined in no prayer groups, no bible study groups, no fellowship groups, nor any other form of church activity.

Martin does not feel at all closely involved in the life of his local church, and what is more, he has no desire to become more involved. Because he has attended no discussion groups, he has not found the opportunity to talk about any specific religious or secular issues with his fellow members of the church. He does not feel that he suffers any lack because of this. He says that he does not want the opportunity to talk about the bible and prayer, sex and marriage, pop music and television, work and unemployment, or politics and society, at least within the context of his church.

Martin has never served on any church committees or helped with the work of his church through undertaking such responsibilities as teaching in a Sunday school or helping with the youth work. Moreover, he is quite adamant that he has no desire to undertake any responsibilities of this nature in the future. He says that he has no desire to sit on any church committees or to undertake any specific work among young people for his church.

Similarly, Martin is not interested in taking any sort of active role in the Sunday services which he attends. Occasionally he is invited to read a lesson, and he accepts the invitation to do so, but he has no desire to read more frequently. Moreover, he is quite clear that he does not want to help with worship in any other ways. He has no desire to help in conducting worship, leading prayers or preaching. He does not want to be involved in preparing for the services, welcoming visitors to the service, giving out books or taking the collection. Nor has he any desire to help with the music or to become involved in liturgical dance or drama. Martin sees his attendance at church as something essentially passive, rather than active.

If Martin were to be given a say in the future development of the life of his church, there are two aspects of church life which he would be personally interested in developing. He reckons that he would like to become more involved in helping people in the local neighbourhood and in the church's missionary work overseas. He says that, if his church gave more emphasis to these two aspects, he would be personally prepared to give some time to them.

Martin also reckons that his local church should give more time to teaching about Christ and about Christianity. He reckons that more time should be given to learning what it means to be a Christian, to learning about prayer and worship, and to co-operating with other churches in the neighbourhood. However, having said this, Martin is quite clear that he would not want to give any of his own time to becoming involved in such matters. He reckons that it would be good for other members of his church to become more involved in these kinds of ways, although he is not interested in joining in himself. Similarly, Martin believes that his church should give more time to the problems of the Third World, but once again he is not interested in taking this issue more seriously himself.

Finally, there are three areas in which Martin believes that it would be wrong for his church to give a higher priority. He considers his church should not be giving more time to campaigning on local issues, or conducting evangelism in the local neighbourhood. Similarly, he considers that his church should not be allocating more time to enable its members to share their thoughts, feelings and problems with each other. Martin seems in favour neither of the evangelistic nor the introspective church.

The last thing that Martin would ever say about the usual Sunday worship of his church is that it is full of life. He finds the services dull, and the sermons boring. He feels that the Sunday services are out of touch with the way young people are today. For this reason, he does not feel that the services have any relevance for his daily life.

Although he feels negatively about the Sunday services, Martin feels much more postively about the minister who conducts them. While the services are out of touch with young people today, the minister is most certainly not out of touch. He is an extremely friendly and approachable person. Martin feels that he really listens to what young people have to say, and they would never dismiss him as old-fashioned or irrelevant. He has a very successful ministry among children. While less successful with teenagers than with younger children, he certainly does not fail in his ministry among teenagers.

In fact the minister of Martin's church seems to have tried to bring his services up-to-date. Generally the services use contemporary language and are quite easy for strangers to understand and to follow. Nevertheless, Martin feels that the older people in his church resent these changes and try to stop the younger people from having too much influence on church policy. Martin feels that there is something of a conflict in his church between the younger people who are keen on change and the older people who do not like change. The result is that the teenagers have had very little say in what happens in the church.

In spite of this tension between the generations, Martin feels that his church is quite a friendly place. There is a good deal of fellowship among the older people, and at the same time there is a good sense of fellowship among the teenage members. Although he feels that the older people do not really value his opinion, he says that they are always friendly towards him. Generally, he feels that the church is an open and welcoming community, which makes vistors welcome. Those who attend his church also seem to mix well in the wider community with those who are not church-goers.

While Martin has been bought up as a Baptist all his life, he has also had some experience of other Christian denominations. He has sometimes attended services in the Church of England, Roman Catholic and Methodist churches. On the other hand, he has had no experience of the other major world faiths, or of other religious groups.

Martin's own religious faith is far from being secure. At the present time, he feels that he is an agnostic rather than a believer. He is no longer at all sure of his faith in God. He is no longer at all sure that he can accept the central notion of Christianity which calls Jesus the Son of God. He has problems with accepting the church's teaching that Jesus really rose from the dead. Studying science subjects at school may have been the cause of his movement away from any fundamentalist views on the biblical teaching about creation. He reckons that the idea that God made the world in six days and rested on the seventh is a load of rubbish. He is no longer willing to believe that Christianity has any form of monopoly on religious truth. He reckons that other religions are just as likely to be true.

Martin says that he has now come to doubt the importance of religion in his own life. Looking back, he cannot remember any occasion at all when he has felt the power of God guiding his life. He has never experienced anything which he would describe as a religious experience. At no time in his life has he really felt a deepening of commitment to Christ or a true religious conversion. Nowadays he has given up the practice of bible reading and never thinks of saying grace before meals. He is no longer convinced that religion should have a part to play in schools.

In spite of his fairly trenchant rejection of much of his Christian upbringing, Martin is far from becoming a thoroughgoing secularist. He is still inhabiting a world which has more than enough room for the supernatural. In a very real sense, he seems to be searching for a faith by which to live. He reads his horoscope regularly and believes in the power of the horoscope to predict the future. He accepts without question the existence of intelligent life on other planets. He firmly believes in the continuation of life after death. Sometimes he finds himself very attracted to theories about reincarnation. Most significantly of all, Martin continues to pray daily, although he is far from sure about the reality or the identity of the God to whom he prays.

Against the background of his Christian upbringing, Martin has developed a character of considerable integrity and openness. He is willing and able to be honest with himself and about himself to others. He is not ashamed to admit when he makes a mistake. He is willing to own up to lying, breaking a promise, or taking things which do not belong to him. He acknowledges that he knows what it is to feel resentment when he fails to get his own way, or jealousy when others seem to get on better than he manages to do himself.

Martin has developed a strict attitude towards the law. He feels that the law should be obeyed and that it is wrong to try to evade the requirements of the law. For example, he is strongly against condoning the sale of cigarettes to children under the legal age. He feels that parking restrictions should be carefully obeyed. He refuses to condone the attempt to travel on public transport without paying the fare.

Because he is under the age of sixteen, Martin completed the shorter version of the attitude inventory. For this reason, our view of his moral attitudes is far from complete. What we are able to say, however, is that, over the limited range of moral issues sampled, Martin seems to be adopting a liberal point of view. For example, he says that he does not consider it to be morally wrong to get drunk. He does not want to take a moral stand against euthanasia. He is not showing concern about issues like the divorce rate or violence on television. Martin believes that moral values are of considerable importance to him. But the moral values he espouses are not necessarily those of traditional Baptist Christianity.

Politics has not begun to play a significant part in Martin's life; so far he has taken very little interest in political issues, and no part at all in political activity. Nevertheless, Martin seems to have inherited a fairly strong set of political views. Without any doubt, Martin is following in Conservative footsteps. He says that he has no confidence whatsoever in the policies of either the Liberal or the Labour parties, but that he has a great deal of confidence in the policies of the Conservative party. And he really believes that it makes a difference which political party is in power. Martin is also very strong in his condemnation of the National Front.

By way of an example of his political views, Martin is very much a Conservative party man in his attitudes towards industry. He reckons that nationalisation is one of the worst possible diasters to hit industrial development. He is very clear that the trade unions now have far too much power, and that the power of the trade unions is largely responsible for industrial ills. For his own part, Martin says that he wants to back home industry by buying British.

On racial matters, Martin says that he feels no prejudice against the ethnic minority groups currently living in England. On the other hand, he is very convinced that future immigration should be severely restricted.

On economic matters, Martin says that he is concerned about the problems caused by inflation, and even more concerned about the problems caused by unemployment. However, he seems to have no real sense of understanding about the cause or nature of these problems. He is quite happy to argue that most unemployed people could have a job if they really wanted to. Martin seems content to blame the unemployed themselves for not working, rather than tackling the root problem of lack of work.

The whole issue of world politics seems too far removed from Martin's own experience for him to want to take such matters at all seriously. He is vaguely aware of what is going in the world, but he is generally left untouched by it all. He sees no point in being concerned about the world situation. After all, he feels that there is nothing which he can do to help solve the world's problems.

Having said all this, Martin is not left untouched by the major issues which confront the world today. He says that he is concerned about the risk of nuclear war. He is concerned about the risk of pollution to the environment. He is concerned about the poverty of the Third World, and about the problems of homelessness. These, according to Martin, are the big questions which ought to worry people today. He is much less concerned about what he would call the less significant problems about which people tend to grumble in his own community, things like the crime rate or the health service.

Martin is happy with his life at school. He enjoys his school work and wants to do well at it. He believes that it is important to work hard, and is quite happy to work hard himself. He finds his school work quite easy and he does not often worry about it. The one thing regarding which Martin is not so happy at school concerns his class-mates. He finds that his own positive attitude towards school is far from shared by many alongside whom he has to work, and sometimes this makes things unpleasant for him.

Away from school, Martin feels that he leads quite a full and happy life. He is never bored for something to do in his leisure time. In the last three months he has been out to the cinema and to discotheques. Although under age, he quite often goes out drinking with his friends in public houses. At home he likes watching the television and listening to music. He reckons that he gets enough of books at school, and so rarely reads at home.

Martin has never become involved with a youth club through his church, but he does belong to a local secular youth club which he attends most weeks. He is not a great sportsman. He does not spend much time watching sport or taking part in sport. Nevertheless, he does belong to a local sports club and spends some of his leisure time there as well.

Overall, Martin says that he finds his life really worth living. He feels that his life has a sense of purpose, and a sense of direction. He is looking forward to growing up into the adult world. He is positive about his future.

Although Martin finds himself disliking some of his class-mates at school, he is himself never short of a friend. He likes to be part of a crowd. He is an outgoing person who likes to do the sort of things that are a little frightening. His friends are very important to him and he takes trouble to keep up with the crowd to which he belongs. Nevertheless, he is an independent person, who will do what he wants to do, irrespective of what the others might say. He is not afraid of what people think of him.

Martin is not an anxious person. He does not worry about his work at school, or about his future. He has no anxiety about his ability to cope with life. He is not worried about his relationships with other people. He does not worry about his health.

Martin wants to be a self-sufficient sort of person. He does not like talking about his personal life with others. He wants to keep his thoughts and his feelings to himself. He feels that he should be able to cope on his own. He does not rely on other people for help or advice. He cannot remember ever having found it helpful to talk about his problems with either his mother or his father. He has never found it helpful to talk about problems with close friends. He has never turned to the minister of his church for help or advice. Nevertheless, he has quite a respect for the minister of his church, and he reckons that, if he should ever need help, his minister would be the first person to whom he would turn.

Seeing Martin in church two or three times a month, his minister might well be likely to think of him as a young man firmly rooted in the faith. This is clearly not the case. Growing up in a secular world, Martin is subject to all the doubts and alternative attractions which militate against his allegiance to Christ and his membership of the church. His links with the church are already tenuous. He lacks the opportunities for personal relationships with other teenage church-goers, the senior members of the congregation and the minister. Although he seems to have a real respect and liking for the minister of his church, it is unlikely that the minister will ever get close enough to Martin to have the chance to work openly and honestly with his growing doubts and difficulties. It is likely that Martin's contact with the Baptist Church has persisted as long as it has solely because of the active commitment of his parents. When Martin finally throws over these parental ties, it is likely that his pattern of church attendance, which has persisted for ten years of his life, will cease, at least for a time. Whether or not Martin is subsequently drawn back into the Baptist Church at a later stage in his life will then depend on factors largely out of the control of his present church.

CAROLE

Carole is a seventeen year old who worships regularly at a new ecumenical centre. The old denominational labels no longer mean very much to her at all. The ecumenical centre brings together Anglicans, Baptists, Methodists and members of the United Reformed Church. Carole describes herself as belonging to all of these four denominations.

Carole has been bought up within a Christian family and has been going to church regularly as long as she can remember. Her parents took her to services with them as a babe in arms and as a toddler. For four years, between the ages of three and six, Carole went along to the Sunday school as well as to church services, but she stopped going to Sunday school when she was seven. She joined the church youth group when she was ten and she has been a regular member ever since. A year later, when she was eleven, Carole joined the church sponsored-guides, and she has regularly attended guide meetings ever since.

Carole comes from a semi-professional home background. Her father taught history and her mother teaches modern languages in a local school. Her father died a few years ago, and is very sadly missed by Carole.

Carole attended a county secondary school where she obtained more than five O levels, mainly in art subjects. Now she attends the local college of further education where she is working for her A levels. She continues to live at home with her mother.

Carole is very closely involved in the life of her church. She rarely lets a Sunday pass without going to a service. Last Sunday she attended three services, two in the morning and one in the evening. She notes that this is rather unusual, although quite often she will attend two Sunday services, one in the morning and one in the evening.

Carole regularly helps in the church services by reading lessons, by giving out the books, or by taking the collection. Sometimes she also leads the prayers, welcomes visitors at the door or makes the coffee after the service. If given the opportunity, Carole would like to take an even more active role in the services. In particular, she would like to be involved in conducting the service, in offering drama within the service, and in assisting with the music by playing an instrument or by singing in a small group. She is not interested in joining the regular choir, taking part in liturgical dance, serving at the altar, or preaching.

As well as belonging to the church youth club and the church-sponsored guides, Carole is also an active member of a house group organised for teenagers. All of these groups give Carole plenty of opportunities to discuss a range of issues within the context of her church. She has recently been able to join in discussions on the bible, television, the environment, politics, the Third World and work. At the same time, she feels her groups should have covered many more areas. She would like her church groups to talk more about prayer, racism, unemployment, law and order, cults like the moonies and personal relationships.

At present Carole helps her church by working as a leader of a children's group. Now she feels that the time is right for her to take on more responsibilities in her church. She would like to be able to serve on the parochial church council, although she has no desire to serve on the deanery synod. She would also like to be able to assist as a Sunday school teacher.

Carole feels that there are a great number of areas in which her church should be more actively involved and she says that she is willing to commit herself to these areas. For example, she believes that her church should give more time to learning what it means to be a Christian, to learning about prayer and worship, and to helping the individual members share their thoughts, feelings and problems. She feels that her church should take a more active part in local evangelism and in the church's missionary work overseas. She feels her church should become more involved in the areas of the Third World, local politics and ecumenism.

Carole has a very positive attitude towards the usual Sunday worship of her church. She feels that the services are usually full of life and in touch with young people today. The services make full use of modern language and she would never accuse them of being boring. She finds the usual Sunday services very relevant for her life today. Nevertheless, the Sunday services do not completely escape without criticism. Often the worst part is the sermon. Sometimes Carole finds the sermon helpful, but not usually. Although Carole has a specific task to perform at some of the services, she often feels more like a spectator than she would like. She often wonders just what strangers would make of her church. She fears that they might well have problems in understanding what is going on and in really joining in.

Carole's views on worship are thoroughly progressive. She is strongly in favour of the modern forms of services. She likes singing modern hymns in church. She is totally in favour of women taking a leading role in worship, and in the ordination of women to the priesthood.

Carole is lucky in belonging to a church where her progressive views are shared by the majority of the congregation. She feels that the other teenagers in the congregation are also in favour of change, and so are the older members of the congregation. Although she does not feel that her own generation has much real influence on church policy, she is not aware of there being a lot of conflict between the various generations of church-goers at the ecumenical centre.

The ecumenical centre is a friendly place. Carole is made to feel at home there both by the older members and by the other teenagers. She also reckons that the church-goers integrate well into the wider local community.

Carole also has a very positive attitude towards her parish priest. She describes him as a very friendly, approachable person, who gets on well with teenagers and with younger children. He is the kind of clergyman who takes young people seriously and has a good ministry among them. He gives the impression of being in touch with life, up-to-date and relevant.

Carole says that her religion is very important to her daily life. It is not something which is confined to Sundays. She tries to take seriously a regular pattern of spirituality. She tries to give some time everyday to private prayer and to bible reading. She says grace before most meals. She is very confident of the power of God guiding her life. Her commitment to God has grown gradually over the years. She can point to no particular moment of conversion, nor to a particular turning point in her life. The sense of the presence of God has simply grown upon her.

Carole has no doubt about her religious beliefs. She is clear about her belief in God. She firmly believes that Jesus really rose from the dead, and that Jesus is the Son of God. She firmly believes in life after death.

She will have no truck with teachings about reincarnation. Carole holds a critical and open attitude towards scripture. Of course she believes in God as the creator of everything, but she does not accept as literally true the Genesis account of God making the world in six days and resting on the seventh. In spite of her firm commitment to Christianity, Carole remains open minded towards the other world faiths. She does not maintain that Christianity is the only true religion. On the other hand, she is quite clear that her commitment to the church should rule out simultaneously holding superstitious beliefs, like belief in her horoscope.

The ecumenical centre gives Carole the feeling of really belonging both to the Church of England and to the Free Churches. Her experience of ecumenism does not, however, stop there. She has also attended Roman Catholic services. Carole has no experience of any other major world faiths or of minority religious movements.

Carole's strong religious faith goes hand in hand with a fairly conservative set of moral values. She believes that it is wrong to have sexual intercourse outside marriage. She believes that family life is being threatened by society's permissive attitude towards divorce. She feels that pornography is morally corrupting. She stands out against abortion. Her conservatism is not complete, however. She finds the idea of contraceptives acceptable. She is not critical of the practice of homosexuality.

While Carole is quite definite about her moral views on issues of sexuality, she is much less clear about her moral views on issues like drugs and alcohol. She says that she is unsure whether to regard the use of marijuana as morally wrong or not. She is unsure of whether it is morally wrong to become drunk or whether drunkenness should be morally acceptable in today's society.

Carole is firmly convinced that law and order should be strictly upheld. She would never condone law-breaking behaviour. The selling of cigarettes to children under the legal age, travelling without a ticket and the infringement of parking restrictions are all to be condemned.

Carole says that she tries hard to live an honest and good life. She is always willing to admit when she makes a mistake. She has never stolen anything in her life. Nevertheless, she is aware of her failings and she is not ashamed to own up to them. She confesses that she has broken promises and told lies. She has taken advantage of people. She has felt jealous when others seem to get a better deal out of life than she does herself. She has felt resentful when she has failed to get her own way. As a committed Christian, Carole feels that she is striving for a higher standard than she has ever reached. But she knows that God will never stop loving her because of her failings. She writes, 'going to church has taught me to try to follow Jesus more closely and it has encouraged me when I have fallen short and felt like giving up'.

Politics is important to Carole, although she has never taken an active part in politics. She believes that it really does make a considerable difference which political party is in power. She gives her own firm vote to the Liberal party. She says that she has a lot of confidence in the policies of the Liberal party. On the other hand, she has no confidence at all in the policies of the Labour party, the Conservative party or the National Front.

On industrial issues, Carole has no firm political views. She has not made up her mind whether the nationalisation of industry is a good thing or not. She has not made up her mind whether she thinks that the trade unions have too much power or not. On social issues, Carole has come to a much firmer conclusion: here she takes a left wing view. She believes that private schools should be abolished and that private medical practice should not be encouraged. On racial issues, Carole stands out very strongly against the statement that there are too many black people living in this country today. She says that it is absurd to say something as prejudiced as this. She does not believe that any restriction should be placed on immigration into Britain in the future.

Carole says that she finds the world situation very disturbing. She is very anxious about the risk of nuclear war. She is very concerned about the risks of pollution to the environment. She is very concerned about the poverty of the Third World and the problems of homelessness. These are issues she takes seriously. She believes that it is worthwhile thinking about these issues and trying to discover what people like her can actually do to help solve the world's problems.

Nearer to home, Carole is aware of the difficulties and problems confronting her own society. She identifies unemployment as the major problem facing England today. She says that it is silly to blame the unemployed for not having a job. The problem goes much deeper than that: the jobs are not there in the first place. She is also concerned about the rate of inflation, and about the rise in the crime rate.

Carole has not enjoyed her transfer from school to the college. She likes her fellow students, but finds that her old school was a happier place to study than the college. Carole is not really ambitious in her study, but she does worry a lot about it. She reckons that she has to work very hard to keep up.

Carole's commitment to her church takes up a lot of her spare time.

Her church is very important to her, and she would be happy for it to take even more of her time. Apart from her commitment to the church, she also belongs to a sports club. She likes watching sport as well as taking an active part in sport herself. She likes going out to the cinema and to the theatre. She does not go out drinking with her friends. At home she likes watching television, listening to music and reading. All told, Carole reckons that she has a full life. She does not long for more things to do in her leisure time.

A number of Carole's friendships were formed through her church. Friends are important to her, and she takes a lot of notice of what they think and say about her. She likes being with her friends, but she does not like being with large crowds of people. She finds crowds oppressive. She needs to feel safe, loved and secure. She does not like doing things that are frightening. Carole is much more of an introvert than an extravert.

Carole often feels depressed. She worries about things far too much. She worries about her work. She is very anxious about her ability to cope. She worries about her relationships with other people. She is very worried about her relationships with boys, and about her sex life. She often feels insecure and unloved. She often doubts her worth as a person.

Carole says that she often longs for someone to turn to for advice. She finds it helpful to talk things over with her mother, but she still misses her father very much. She often talks about her feelings with close friends and she finds this very helpful. She writes, 'I have many friends at church. And when I am depressed the services and people at church help me to feel better'. Most of all, however, she feels that she is able to turn to her parish priest. He has been a great help to her.

Carole is a young lady who receives a lot of help from her church. She is also one who is very willing to work hard for her church. She is lucky in belonging to a church which is able both to respond to her needs and to give her the opportunity to grow in her faith. With this kind of pastoral care, Carole stands a good chance of remaining a faithful and useful teenage member of her church, and of growing into an adult church member.

DAVID

David is a nineteen year old member of the Church of England. He has been attending church services regularly since the age of four. He joined the Church of England Sunday school when he was five and continued to go to Sunday school as well as to church services until the age of ten. At ten years of age he transferred from the Sunday school to the church youth club. He is still a regular member of this youth club. The church which David attends also sponsors a scout group. He joined this church-sponsored scout group at the age of eleven and kept his membership going for three or four years.

David was prepared for confirmation when he was twelve. He attended confirmation classes for nearly six months before being confirmed. David has now become a very loyal supporter of his local church. Very rarely does a Sunday pass without David attending at least one service. Last Sunday, for example, he attended a mid-morning communion service as well as an evening service of Evensong. The church which David attends is one which attracts quite a number of young people. He reckons there were at least thirty other teenagers at the holy communion service he attended last Sunday.

Although David's parents used to take him to church as a child, and made sure that he went to Sunday school from the age of five, his parents are by no means as committed to the church as he is. David continues to go to church by himself without much by way of parental support or encouragement.

David left school when he was sixteen, after obtaining four CSEs and two or three O levels. At school he says that his strengths were in art subjects rather than scientific subjects. He attended a county secondary school, not one run in association with the Church of England. After leaving school he has not attempted to go on to gain any further qualifications. Now he works as a clerical assistant for the Department of Health and Social Security. He continues to live at home with his parents. He comes from a semi-professional home background. His father works as a financial director with quite a large firm. His mother has never worked outside the home.

One of David's major links with his local church has arisen through the church choir. David enjoys singing and is very glad to belong to the choir. He reckons that this is one of the incentives to attend Evensong most weeks as well as the regular morning service. His membership of the choir gives David an important sense of having something worthwhile to offer to the worship of his church. He is occasionally able to contribute to the service in other ways as well. From time to time, he is asked to read a lesson. He is part of a small group of singers who are invited occasionally to sing at services. He belongs to the liturgical drama group which presents something in the services at least once a month.

If given the opportunity, David would be keen to take an even more active part in the services of his local church. He would like to extend his musical contribution to playing an instrument in a church music group. He would like to help with the offertory and to act as a sidesman responsible for welcoming visitors. He would like to be helped to preach in church.

Although he takes an active part in the Sunday services, and belongs to the youth club, David has no other involvement with his local church. He belongs to no study groups or discussion groups, and he has no desire to do. He appreciates the fellowship of the church youth club, but does not see that group as somewhere in which he wants to talk about religion. He says that he has never joined in church discussions on the bible or prayer, sex or marriage, politics or television, and he has no desire to do so now.

Similarly, David has never taken a part in the committees responsible for various aspects of the life of his church. Again, he says that he has no desire to become involved in things like the church social committee, the parochial church council or the deanery synod. He has never been involved in teaching in the Sunday school or in running the youth club. Again, he says that he would not want to become involved in the formal Sunday school, but he would be willing to take a leadership role in doing something less formal and less regular for children.

Assessing his current commitment to the church, David is very content with the existing priorities. There are no areas of church life into which he feels he ought to be directing more of his energy. He does not want to become more involved as a disciple, learning more about worship, prayer or the Christian way of life. He does not want to become more involved as an apostle, being sent out to help those in need and to proclaim the gospel to those who do not come to church. On the other hand, David does feel that his church should be making more opportunities for others to become more involved in the life and witness of the church. For example, he feels that his church should give a higher priority to becoming involved in the church's missionary work overseas, and to becoming more aware of Third World problems. He feels that there should be more opportunities for learning about prayer and worship, and for learning what it means to be a Christian in today's world.

Although he enjoys the music of his church very much, David has to admit that many people would find the services difficult to follow and far from rewarding. Personally he likes modern services, but he would never be able to describe the services he attends each Sunday as really modern. He feels that there is something old-fashioned and irrelevant about the church. He says that the usual Sunday worship of his church is out of touch with young people today. It seems to lack life and might even be called boring. He is none too sure whether the sermons are helpful to him or not really helpful at all.

David's own views on worship combine a blend of the conservative with the progressive. He likes the use of modern language for the readings from the bible, for the prayers and for the order of service. On the other hand, he has never grown to like modern hymns. As a chorister he much prefers the good music on which he has been brought up. He is far from conservative, however, in his views on the place of women in the church: he is firmly infavour of women priests. Generally David feels that the other people in his church are more conservative in their taste than he is himself. He feels that the older church-goers are very resistant to change, and he is far from sure that the younger church-goers are any more open to change than the older ones. While he feels that the teenagers do not have much influence on church policy, he reckons that things would look much the same if they did.

David feels that his church is a friendly place. He says that the older people in his church are friendly towards each other, and friendly towards him as a teenager. He feels that the teenage church-goers are a friendly bunch as well. He also describes the vicar as a friendly person.

When David describes his vicar as a friendly person, this emerges as the one positive thing he feels able to say about him. David is not actually critical of the vicar of his church, but he gives the impression that the vicar leaves a lot to be desired. For example, he could not really say that the vicar is actually good with either children or teenagers. He never really gives the impression of being up-to-date or in touch with life. David says that you can never be sure that he is taking you seriously and hearing rightly what you are trying to say.

David feels very sure of his religious faith. He has no doubts about his belief in God or about his belief in Jesus Christ. He has no hesitation in affirming his faith that Jesus really rose from the dead and that he is the Son of God. David knows where he stands in relationship to belief in life after death. He firmly believes that death is not the end, and he refuses to have anything to do with non-Christian views of life after death involving notions like reincarnation. His views on creation are less clear. He feels uncomfortable with the Genesis story that God made the world in six days and rested on the seventh, but he is unwilling to dismiss this account out of hand. David believes that religious education should be taught in schools. He is firmly convinced that

Christianity is the only true religion. He is not a superstitious person: he has no time for things like his horoscope.

David says that his religion plays an important part in his life. He does not, however, allow his religious practice to spread far beyond Sundays. He would never think, in the normal course of events, of attending a mid-week church service, unless something very special was happening. He has no regular discipline of private prayer or of bible reading. He says that he prays and reads the bible when he feels like it. When pressed, he says that he does not feel like it very often, and certainly less than once a month. He never says grace before meals.

Looking back over his life, David does not feel that there has been any particular turning point or conversion experience which radically changed his commitment to Christ or to the church. He does not really feel that he has ever had something which he would describe as a religious experience, although he does not rule the possibility completely out of court. On the other hand, he does feel that there have been points in his life when it seemed as if the hand of God was guiding him. He is not completely certain about this, but feels that it is more than probably true.

During the time that he has been a member of the Church of England, David has had limited experience of Christian ecumenism. He has attended services arranged by the Churches of Christ and by the Salvation Army. He has never been to any other churches, like the Baptist, Methodist or Roman Catholic churches. He has had no experience of any of the other major world faiths or of any other religious movements.

Just as David's attitudes towards worship hold in tension a blend between the traditional and the modern, so his moral attitudes hold in tension a blend between the conservative and the liberal. David has developed a permissive attitude towards heterosexual and homosexual behaviour. He does not consider that it is wrong to have sexual intercourse outside marriage. He does not consider the practice of homosexuality to be wrong. He accepts contraception as morally right. He is not worried about the availability of pornography, or the lack of censorship on television. On the other hand, he is worried by the social trends in divorce: he believes that divorce is becoming too easy and that family life is being undervalued by today's society. He is also highly critical of abortion and euthanasia. David argues that it is highly wrong to become drunk, but he sees nothing wrong in the use of marijuana.

David regards himself as a highly law-abiding citizen. He disagrees strongly with any suggestion that the law does not matter, or that it is reasonable to try to get away with breaking the law. He reckons that it is a serious matter to try to travel on public transport without buying a ticket. He reckons that selling cigarettes to children under the legal age is an equally serious offence. He takes a more lenient attitude towards those who leave their car in no-waiting areas, but he is certainly not willing to openly condone such disregard of the law.

David's own integrity is high. He has a good degree of insight into his behaviour and motives. He knows that he is far from perfect, and he is not ashamed to admit his feelings either to himself or to others. He does not try to pretend that he has never lied or broken a promise. He admits to having taken the occasional thing which does not belong to him. He is willing to own up to feelings of resentment and jealously. He knows that he sometimes takes advantage of people. He always tries to admit when he makes a mistake.

Politically, David supports the Liberal party. He says that he has no confidence in the policies of the Labour party, and even less in the policies of the Conservative party and of the National Front. He reckons that the country would be a much better place if only the Liberals held the power in government. David says that politics is important to him, although he would never find himself taking a really active part in politics.

On social issues, like education and the health service, David takes a very left-wing stand. He believes that private schools should be abolished and that private medical practice should not be encouraged. On racial issues, David takes a very right-wing view. Not only does he believe that immigration into Britain should be restricted, he also says that he reckons there are already too many black people living in this country. David is quite racially prejudiced. On industrial issues, David is far from sure where to take his stand. He says he cannot make up his mind whether the nationalisation of industry is a good thing or not. Similarly, he cannot make up his mind whether the trade unions use their power wisely or not.

David does not find himself very interested in the wider issues of world politics. He feels that there is little point in becoming too concerned about the world situation because there is nothing that he can do to help solve the world's problems. David tends to feel rather apathetic and powerless in relationship to the things that really matter in today's world. Of course, he is concerned about the risk of nuclear war. But what, he asks, is the point of being concerned if he cannot do anything about the situation? He prefers to turn a blind eye to major issues like the pollution of the environment, the poverty of the Third World, the problems of homelessness and the crime rate.

Nearer to home, David finds the rate of inflation a matter of concern. After all, inflation continues to erode the value of his own pay-packet. On the other hand, he registers no concern for the large number of people who are unemployed. After all, he has a job himself. Moreover, he has no real sympathy for the unemployed: he feels that most of them could have a job if they really wanted one.

David is very happy in his job with the Department of Health and Social Security, and he likes the people with whom he works. He is willing to work hard, and he would like to get promotion. Sometimes he finds himself worrying about his work, but he tries not to worry about it too much. He does not feel that his present job is well paid, but it is secure, and money is not all that important to him anyway.

In his leisure time, David either goes along to the church youth club, or down to the pub with his friends. Within the past three months he has not been out to engage in any other form of leisure activity. In fact, he says that he is spending an increasing amount of his time and a bigger part of his wages in the pub than he used to. David is no sportsman. He is content to watch sport on the television, but he would never dream of going out to watch sport. He is even less interested in taking an active part in sport himself. At home, apart from watching television, David listens to a lot of music and does a little reading. Generally, he is very happy with the ways in which he spends his leisure time. He says that he does not wish for more things to do when he is not at work. He reckons that his leisure time is adequately occupied.

On the surface, David says that he is making out alright in life. Usually he finds life worth living, and certainly his church gives him a sense of purpose. Underneath it all, however, David is a rather insecure and lonely young man. He has not much confidence in himself. He needs friends very much, and he is easily hurt if they reject him. He likes being with people, but often finds that being part of a crowd gets on top of him. He often finds himself worrying about his relationships with other people, especially with girls. He does not feel that he is worth all that much as a person, and he cannot really understand why people should bother to take him seriously. He often finds himself worrying about his health, about his ability to cope with life, and about the risks of having a breakdown. In fact he often feels depressed, although never so depressed that he doubts the value of going on living.

Certainly when he feels depressed, David needs the help and support of others. He knows that in this situation it is useless to try to talk with his father, and talking to his mother is not much better. It is here that close friends have been a help to David, especially the friends he has made through his church. But most of all, he has valued talking to a clergyman. He does not find the present vicar of his church much help, but he had a good relationship with the previous vicar, and he reckons that this made all the difference to his life. He writes about a specific problem he faced in the past that 'if it was not for my religion I would have had no one to turn to'. He remembers that occasion and he hopes that other teenagers may come to benefit from the church in the same way as he has done himself.

David is one of those young people to whom the church has been a great help. He has stuck with the church through to the end of his teenage years. In many ways, he would now like gradually to draw others into the community he has valued. It is important that his local church should understand this and give him both the opportunity for growing in his faith and the security to enable him to take the risks inevitably involved in any such process of growth.

MARY

Mary is an eighteen year old Roman Catholic from the city of Lancaster. She comes from a strong Roman Catholic family where care has been taken to see that she too should be brought up in the faith. For as long as she can remember, Mary has been going to church on a Sunday, and she received all her schooling within Roman Catholic voluntary aided schools. Mary was confirmed within the Roman Catholic Church when she was eleven.

Mary left school after obtaining five O levels. Then she went on to take a secretarial course at college. Now she is employed as a clerical assistant within British Telecom. She continues to live at home with her parents. The social background of Mary's home is that of socio-economic class three. Her father works as a telephone engineer. Her mother works as a cashier in a shop.

Mary has remained a loyal Sunday worshipper at her church, although she no longer goes to church every Sunday without fail. Nowadays she finds that there are a number of other attractions competing for her precious free time on a Sunday. Nevertheless, you are likely to find Mary in church on two or three Sundays every month. Last Sunday she got up late and went to a midday mass. None of her family or friends were going to this late morning service themselves, so

Mary went alone. She knew that once she had arrived at church she would be in the company of a number of young people of her own age. In fact, last Sunday there were thirty of forty other teenagers in the congregation as well as Mary herself.

Mary sees her church membership very much in terms of attending mass on a Sunday and little else. She never thinks, for example, of going to a weekday service, or of attending any church-based groups, arranged either specifically for young people or for people of all ages. She has been to no form of church study group or social group within the past three months. She has taken part in no church discussion groups within the past three months. She is quite clear that these kind of things do not appeal to her and that she has no desire to join them in the future.

Moreover, when Mary goes to mass on a Sunday, she does not expect to take any responsibility for the organisation or running of the service. She is usually content to sit back and to leave the more active participation to others. She has accepted no regular responsibilities or functions within her local church. Occasionally Mary will read a lesson, or join the choir for a special service. Once or twice she has taken part in liturgical dance or drama in church. She is reluctant to do more than this in a service. She says that she does not want to help with conducting worship, leading the prayers, serving at the altar, or preaching. Although she enjoys joining the choir on occasions, she would not want to become more involved in a young persons' music group. If Mary was really pressed to choose some way of assisting in the service, the one thing which she would consider undertaking is making the coffee afterwards.

Mary is not the sort of person who likes to serve on committees. She has never served on any of the local or area committees of her church, and she has no desire to do so in the future. If she was pressed to help with the work of her local church, she would rather try her hand at work with children or young people rather than sit on a committee. Although she has had no experience of doing such things in the past, Mary says that she would quite like to try her hand at becoming a leader of the children's or young people's group. However, she is far from convinced that such opportunities are likely to come her way in her local church.

Looking to the future, Mary feels that there are things to which her church should be giving higher priority and in which she would personally be willing to become involved. She says that she would be willing to give more time to co-operating with other churches in the neighbourhood, to becoming aware of the problems of the Third World, and to learning more about prayer and worship. She also feels that her church should give greater opportunities for the young members to share their thoughts, feelings and problems, although personally she would not wish to become more involved in this kind of way. On the other hand, Mary does not feel that her local church should give more time to helping people in the neighbourhood, to campaigning on local issues, to conducting evangelism in the local area, or to becoming more involved in the church's missionary work overseas.

Mary has been attending the same church for a number of years and she has built-up a valuable set of friendships with the other young people of her own age who also worship there on Sundays. She feels that these teenagers are a likeable and friendly group of people. They get on well with each other, and they get on well with other young people who do not attend church.

On the other hand, Mary does not feel so positively towards the older people who worship in her church. She feels that the older members of the congregation have built up a set of relationships among themselves to the exclusion of welcoming young people to their number. She feels that the older people ignore her and her friends when they come to church. According to Mary, the older members of the congregation are responsible for making all the important decisions that affect church life, and they flatly refuse to take into account the views of the younger church-goers. For this reason, she reckons that the teenagers in her church are completely unable to influence church policy. The real conflict comes, she says, when the young church-goers want changes and the older church-goers refuse to accept change.

Because the older people in Mary's church refuse to accept change, she feels that the usual Sunday services remain old-fashioned. She says that she finds the Sunday services she attends boring and lifeless. She complains that they fail to actively involve the congregation. Although she still attends services quite regularly, she finds that they have tended to become irrelevant to her daily life. She reckons that the sermons are generally dull and uninteresting. The preacher does not usually have anything to say that Mary finds helpful.

At the end of her questionnaire Mary comments on this problem in greater detail, 'the church, I think, needs to be a more interesting place, in other words I feel that the attendance at the mass would be far greater if the prayers and sermon were shorter and not to strict time, because during the mass everyone knows what is coming next and when. The mass, to me, sounds like it is being read without any feeling or meaning'.

Although Mary is highly critical of the worship provided by her church, she still remains very conservative in her own preferences and attitudes towards worship. Although she criticises the services she attends for being old-fashioned, she is far from sure that she really approves of liturgical change. She is doubtful about the use of modern language in services. She dislikes modern hymns. She is unsure about the acceptability of the ordination of women to the priesthood within the church.

Mary has a more positive attitude towards her parish priest than towards the worship of the church for which he is responsible. She finds her parish priest to be an approachable person. He seems to listen to what people have to say to him, and he seems to be in touch with life today. He is a friendly person who tries to take young people seriously. Nevertheless, Mary feels that he is often out of his depth when trying to deal with children and young teenagers. He sometimes comes over to them as old-fashioned and as irrelevant.

Mary's spirituality seems to be very church-based and restricted to Sundays. She has no regular discipline of private prayer. She says that she prays when she feels the need, perhaps on average about once a week. She rarely reads the bible, and never says grace before meals. She is far from certain about the part played by God in her daily life. She thinks that she may be able to point to times in her life when she has been aware of God's guidance, but she is not really certain. There may have been occasions when she has been conscious of a religious experience, but she is far from sure. In fact, she confesses that her religion is not at all important to her.

Having been brought up as a Roman Catholic, Mary has had little experience of other religious communities. She has never come into contact with any of the other world faiths, she has never experienced any of the other religious movements or sects. In fact, the only other main-line Christian denomination of which she has any experience is the Church of England. For example, she has never been to a service in a Methodist or Baptist church. Inspite of this limited experience, Mary does not seem narrow-minded in her outlook. She feels that her church should be giving much more time to ecumenical work among the Christian denominations. Moreover, she does not believe it right to claim that Christianity has a monopoly of all religious truth.

Mary's religious beliefs are not quite as orthodox as her church might wish. She is confident about her belief in God, but she is far from orthodox in the beliefs she holds about Jesus. She says that she cannot really accept the traditional formulation of the church which calls Jesus the Son of God, although she has no hesitation in accepting the truth of the resurrection of Jesus from the dead. She is confident about her belief in the after-life, but again she is far from orthodox in the precise views she holds about the after-life. She says that she finds no contradiction in holding a belief in reincarnation alongside her Catholic faith.

Mary is far from being a fundamentalist in her views on scripture. She happily accepts the idea of God as creator, but equally happily rejects the Genesis story of the way in which creation took place.

Superstition is something which Mary tries to rule firmly out of her life. She sometimes reads her horoscope out of curiosity, but she claims that she never puts any faith in what it says. She rejects the force of luck in her life. She rules out the possibility of there being intelligent life on other planets.

Moral values are important to Mary, and she has given considerable care and thought to the moral views which she has adopted. She is very aware that her church would thoroughly disapprove of the moral values which she has come to hold. Mary has accepted a liberal view on sexual ethics. She no longer believes that it is wrong to have sexual intercourse outside marriage. She is no longer willing to condemn the practice of homosexuality as morally wrong. She is very clear of her rejection of her church's teaching on contraception.

On this issue of contraception, Mary comments, 'I think the church would be a better place if it opened its views and widened its outlook on general affairs and religions. It seems to pressure young people into believing one thing which in today's society is too difficult. The young people of today are torn between views. A good example is the use of contraceptives, they are told by the church not to use them, but society produces adverts and doctors pressurise people to take precautions, and what happens if because of medical reasons a young girl has to go on the pill? She feels she has let her church and her religion down.'

Mary is also critical of her church's view on abortion. Personally she finds the idea of abortion morally acceptable. Similarly, she is willing to accept the idea of euthanasia. Drugs and alcohol are also areas in which Mary is willing to take a liberal view. She does not consider it morally wrong to become drunk or to use drugs like marijuana.

In spite of adopting a personal set of moral values so far removed from the expectations of her church, Mary is far from happy with the generally permissive nature of the moral climate of the society in which she lives. She feels that British society has swung too far in the direction of moral liberalism. She is critical of the social availability of pornography. She is critical of society's free acceptance of divorce. She is critical of the lack of censorship on television.

While impatient with the moral restrictions imposed by her church, Mary is not generally impatient with the legal restrictions imposed by society. She argues that such things as parking restrictions should be strictly obeyed. She comes down severely against those who attempt to dodge paying their fare on public transport. She is unwilling to approve the illegal sale of cigarettes to children under the legal age.

Mary has a great deal of personal integrity, and considerable insight into her own character. She knows that she is a long way from being perfect, and she is not ashamed to own up to her failings. She freely admits sometimes to having broken promises and to having told lies. She knows that she is far from being immune to feelings of jealousy or to feelings of resentment. Sometimes she has taken advantage of people. She knows when she is in the wrong, and she knows too that she is not always willing to admit when she has made a mistake.

Politics is almost a closed book as far as Mary is concerned. She has never taken an active interest in politics, and finds the whole area irrelevant and boring. She says that she has no confidence in the policies of any of the major political parties. In fact, she reckons that it makes no difference at all which political party is in power.

When questioned in greater detail, Mary reveals that she has formed no particular views on a number of political issues, while on other specific issues she holds a strange mixture of left-wing and right-wing perspectives. For example, on the industrial front, she takes a right-wing view on the corruption of trade unions, but has no views one way or another on the question of the nationalisation of industry. On a social front, she takes a left-wing view on the abolition of private schools, but has no views one way or another on the question of private medical practice. On the issue of racial harmony, she feels that immigration restrictions should be enforced, but she shows no signs of prejudice against minority ethnic communities already established in Britain. Moreover, she is clear that she has no time for the policies and activities of the National Front.

Mary says that she is not particularly concerned about the world situation, but that she is concerned about some of the more immediate problems which confront life in today's world. At the top of her list of world problems she places the twin threats that confront civilisation: the risk of nuclear war and the pollution of the environment. Slightly lower on her list, she places matters which threaten Western prosperity or world development.

At home, Mary feels that inflation and lawlessness are the two biggest problems. By way of comparison, she feels that unemployment is a much less pressing problem. She accepts the fact that work is in short supply and that most unemployed people need to adjust to the idea that they are likely to be out of work for some time. She does not feel that anything can be done about this situation. Further from home, Mary says that she is concerned about the problems of the economic development of the Third World. Again, however, she says that she feels completely powerless to do anything to help solve such problems.

Mary is personally very happy with her job as a clerical assistant within British Telecom. She likes both her work and the people with whom she works. Her work is not a source of worry or anxiety to her. She says that she wants to progress up the promotional ladder at work and that she is willing to work hard. She counts herself lucky to have found a job she likes, given the large unemployment problem in Lancashire. She says that earning her own living is important to her. Even if she were not happy in her job, she says that she would much rather have some sort of work than be on the dole as many of her friends are.

When not at work, Mary enjoys her leisure time in a variety of ways. Sport is one of her major interests, both as a participant activity and as a spectator pastime. She belongs to a local sports centre and spends quite a lot of her spare time there. She is also a member of a local dancing school, and she likes going out to discotheques. Mary often goes drinking with her friends in her leisure time, and is to be found both in the local coffee bars and in the local public houses. She belongs to an evening class and likes going to the cinema. At home, she likes reading, listening to music and watching television. In fact, she says that her leisure time is very fully occupied.

All told, Mary says that she finds life really worth living. She feels that she has a sense of purpose in life. She has a number of good friends and rarely feels lonely. Mary likes to have a lot of people around her. She is very happy when she is part of a crowd of friends. She takes her friendships seriously. What her friends think about her is of considerable importance to her.

Mary has quite a lot of confidence in herself as a person and in her ability to cope with life. She says that she does not really have time to feel depressed or anxious about things. In fact, Mary seems to worry about very little at present. Her work is not a source of worry to her. She has no anxieties about her relationships or about her sex life. She is not worried about her physical or mental health.

Although she is generally a self-sufficient sort of person, Mary realises that she sometimes needs to draw upon the help and support of others. She has tried going to her parents for help and advice, but she no longer feels that they are able to understand her needs. She has tried talking with her parish priest, but has not found that helpful either, and she says that she would not turn to her parish priest for help again. When Mary needs help and advice nowadays, it is to the friends of her own age that she turns, and it is from her friends that she derives the help and support she needs.

At present Mary is probably regarded by her parish priest as a loyal young member of the Roman Catholic Church. Her faith, however, is very superficial and far from secure. She is living a full, happy and successful life in the secular world. She is fully aware of the conflicts and tensions between the faith of her childhood and the aspirations of her adult life. It is probably the case that Mary is an eighteen year old who is unlikely to remain much longer in the household of faith, unless her local church can become much more aware of her needs and flexible enough to speak to them.

12 DISCUSSION

This study has marshalled a great deal of detailed evidence and information about teenage church-goers today. The real job for evidence of this nature is to stimulate further discussion and to facilitate informed debate. If this research is to be useful, it needs now to be used by the local churches and by all of us who have a concern for the church's work among young people.

With this end in mind, instead of finishing with a summary of my own conclusions, I have organised a list of the key questions raised in my mind by each chapter. I hope that this final section will become the vehicle through which local churches will be able to assess their own work among teenagers and to plan realistically for their future work.

Chapter 1 Introduction

1   What is the age structure of your own church congregation, and how do teenagers fit into this?
2   What do you reckon motivates the teenagers who continue to attend your own church?

Chapter 2 Research Design

3   How would your church respond if it were invited to participate in a research project?
4   How acceptable is it to question younger teenagers about their views on issues like human sexuality and drug abuse?
5   Why might some churches be so reluctant to participate in a research project of this nature?

Chapter 3 Teenage Church-goers

6   Why do more girls attend church than boys, and what are the implications of this for the church?
7   Why do older teenagers stop going to church, and how should the churches respond to this?

8   Why are the Roman Catholic Church and the Free Churches better at retaining their older teenagers than the Church of England?

9   How important are church schools in fostering teenage church-goers, and why should there be such an apparent difference between Church of England schools and Roman Catholic schools?

10   Why do teenage church-goers tend to come from the higher social class backgrounds, and what are the implications of this for the churches?

11   How can the churches best relate to the different needs of teenagers who are 1) at school, college or university, 2) engaged in a variety of jobs, or 3) unemployed?

12   How can the churches build bridges between committed teenage church-goers and casual attenders?

13   How important to teenage church-goers is the support of family and friends?

14   What is the significance of admission to adult church membership, and what is the best age for such admission to take place?

15   How important is a special programme of training before admission to adult membership?

16   What should be the role of groups such as church youth clubs and young people's study groups?

17   How successfully can teenagers be integrated into house groups, study groups, etc, organised primarily for adults?

Chapter 4 Church Membership

18   What opportunities does your own church give for teenagers to perform some active role in services?

19   What opportunities does your own church give for teenagers to undertake tasks of responsibility in the church?

20   To what extent should teenagers be involved as Sunday school teachers or the leaders of children's or young people's groups?

21   What topics are teenagers encouraged to discuss within your own church?

22   What is the relationship between the priorities of your church and the views of the teenage members?

Chapter 5 Public Worship

Chapter 6 Religious Beliefs

Chapter 7 Moral Attitudes

the disparity between Christian standards and the standards of the society in which they live?

38 How can teenagers be helped to explore the relationship between their faith and the law?

39 How can teenagers be helped to explore the relationship between their faith and their personal integrity?

Chapter 8 Politics and Society

40 To what extent and in what ways should the churches be involved in the political education of their teenage members?

41 What are the implications for the churches of the way in which, according to the present data, the three denominational groups are aligned with different political parties?

42 How can the churches best help teenagers to explore issues like pollution and nuclear arms?

43 How can the churches best help teenagers to explore issues concerned with the Third World?

44 How can the churches best help teenagers to understand and to respond to the problems of unemployment?

Chapter 9 Work and Leisure

45 How can the churches best help teenagers to cope with the pressures of school, college, university or work?

46 In the case of the teenagers who attend your own church, how does their church membership relate to their other leisure and recreational pursuits?

47 What provision does your own church make for the leisure time of its teenage members?

48 Should the churches attempt to provide a range of leisure activities for their teenage members, or encourage them to make full use of other local secular provision?

Chapter 10 Well-being and Worry

49 How aware is your church of the psychological well-being of its teenage members?

50 How can the churches best respond to the needs of their teenage members if they are depressed, despondent or suicidal?

51 How can the churches help their teenage members to cope with

adolescent feelings of self-doubt, anxiety, loneliness, relationship problems, and so on?

52   How can the churches best respond to the teenagers' needs for approval, acceptance and friendship?

53   How can the churches best develop the counselling skills of the clergy and lay church leaders in ways appropriate to the needs of teenage church-goers?

APPENDIX

APPENDIX: READY REFERENCE TABLES

The ready reference tables are designed to provide an easy summary of some of the statistics on which the text is based. All the salient statistics have been quoted in the text to obviate frequent cross referencing between the chapters and an appendix. However, the tables have been numbered in chapter sequence to facilitate cross referencing if the reader should so desire. Moreover, the attitude statements in the tables have been listed in the precise order in which they are discussed within the chapter. Limitations on space mean that the summary statistics for the attitude statements are presented only in relationship to the two age groups. Detailed sex and denominational breakdowns are given in the text only. In using these tables it needs to be remembered that the percentages have been rounded to the nearest whole numbers. This means that some rows will add up to 99 or 101: it also means that occasionally the aggregated figures reported in the text may differ from those aggregated figures which can be computed from the tables by one percentage point.

Table 2.1   Churches included in the survey by denomination

Denomination	Churches approached N	Participating churches N	Response rate %
Church of England	60	42	70
Roman Catholic	39	22	56
Methodist	29	9	31
United Reformed	9	7	80
Baptist	8	4	50
Salvation Army	3	2	67
Society of Friends	3	3	100
Ecumenical Centre	1	1	100

Table 2.2   Teenagers attending church by denomination

Denomination	Churches N	Teenagers N	Average Number of teenagers per Church
Church of England	42	659	16
Roman Catholic	22	1003	46
Methodist	9	93	10
United Reformed	7	68	10
Baptist	4	47	12
Salvation Army	2	6	3
Society of Friends	3	8	3
Ecumenical Centre	1	18	18

Table 3.1   Teenagers completing the questionnaire

Description		N
Total Group		1328
13-15 year olds	total	720
(by sex)	boys	292
	girls	426
(by denomination)	Free Church	87
	Church of England	283
	Roman Catholic	318
16-20 year olds	total	608
(by sex)	boys	244
	girls	363
(by denomination)	Free Church	88
	Church of England	172
	Roman Catholic	322

Table 5.1 Public Worship

	13-15 year olds					16-20 year olds				
	AS%	A%	NC%	D%	DS%	AS%	A%	NC%	D%	DS%
The usual Sunday worship of my church is boring	10	26	21	35	8	10	27	16	35	12
The usual Sunday worship of my church is full of life	9	27	24	32	8	7	28	17	37	11
The usual Sunday worship of my church is irrelevant to my life	3	12	44	33	8	4	12	22	47	15
Usually I find sermons helpful	5	28	34	23	10	8	38	24	22	8
The usual Sunday worship of my church treats you as a spectator	3	15	39	35	8	4	19	27	40	10
The usual Sunday worship of my church is easy for a stranger to join in	14	54	18	11	3	7	52	21	16	4
The usual Sunday worship of my church is out of touch with young people today	4	26	29	34	7	6	28	22	35	9
I prefer church services that use modern language	24	50	19	6	1	24	50	17	7	2
I like modern hymns in church	22	52	13	10	3	22	52	11	11	4
The usual Sunday worship of my church is modern	4	33	26	30	7	4	32	20	37	7
The 13-20 year olds in my church refuse to accept change	1	3	35	41	20	1	1	22	53	23
The older people in my church refuse to accept change	6	20	47	23	4	8	23	39	26	4
I am in favour of women ministers/priests	12	26	32	16	15	13	27	22	18	19
The minister (vicar) of my church is friendly	42	51	5	3	0	34	58	4	4	0
The minister (vicar) of my church is out of touch with life	3	7	20	43	27	2	7	14	45	31

Table 5.1 Public Worship (continued)

	13-15 year olds					16-20 year olds				
	AS%	A%	NC%	D%	DS%	AS%	A%	NC%	D%	DS%
The minister (vicar) of my church is old fashioned	5	9	19	46	21	4	10	18	48	21
The minister (vicar) of my church is approachable	16	57	20	5	2	19	59	12	8	2
The minister (vicar) of my church is good with teenagers	31	46	16	6	1	25	49	16	9	1
The minister (vicar) of my church is good with children	35	48	11	5	1	26	53	15	5	1
The minister (vicar) of my church ignores what young people have to say	2	5	20	45	28	2	5	20	51	23
The older people in my church are friendly to each other	22	58	15	4	1	15	59	18	6	1
The older people in my church are friendly to me	17	59	18	5	1	14	60	17	7	2
The older people in my church like young people to have a part in making decisions	8	30	45	12	5	4	25	46	18	7
The 13-20 year olds in my church influence church policy	2	13	59	20	7	2	13	38	36	11
The 13-20 year olds in my church are friendly to each other	17	62	16	5	0	14	66	14	5	1
The 13-20 year olds in my church are friendly to me	22	62	13	3	1	19	67	10	3	1
The 13-20 year olds in my church mix well with young people who don't come to church	23	55	19	2	1	23	57	17	3	0

KEY AS   agree strongly
A   agree
NC   not certain
D   disagree
DS   disagree strongly

Table 6.1 Religious Beliefs

	13-15 year olds					16-20 year olds				
	AS%	A%	NC%	D%	DS%	AS%	A%	NC%	D%	DS%
Religion is important to me	23	42	27	7	1	35	37	18	7	2
I think religious education should be taught in school	30	48	15	5	2	30	52	11	5	2
I believe in God	55	30	12	2	1	63	24	10	2	1
I believe that Jesus Christ is the Son of God	62	25	11	1	1	66	21	10	2	1
I believe that Jesus really rose from the dead	49	27	20	3	1	55	24	18	3	1
I believe in life after death	29	26	32	9	5	36	29	26	6	3
I believe that God made the world in six days and rested on the seventh	21	17	31	16	14	20	18	27	17	19
I think Christianity is the only true religion	20	23	29	20	8	26	20	25	19	10
I believe in reincarnation	11	13	41	17	18	10	11	36	19	24
I believe in my horoscope	4	15	26	32	22	3	11	26	30	30
I am concerned about the possibility of an invasion from outer space	2	6	24	34	34	1	5	17	38	39
I believe there is intelligent life on other planets	10	22	42	15	11	11	24	43	13	9
There is really no such think as luck	5	13	26	41	15	6	15	26	40	12

Table 7.1 Moral Attitudes

	13-15 year olds					16-20 year olds				
	AS%	A%	NC%	D%	DS%	AS%	A%	NC%	D%	DS%
Moral values are important to me	20	38	38	3	2	33	50	14	3	0
I think contraception is wrong						5	5	14	36	40
I think it is wrong to have sexual intercourse outside marriage						21	14	15	31	19
I think the practice of homosexuality is wrong						27	15	27	22	9
I think it is wrong to become drunk	18	23	25	23	11	13	26	22	30	10
I think it is wrong to use marijuana (hash or pot)						32	31	18	13	5
I think all war is wrong	42	21	18	12	7	38	23	23	13	4
I think abortion is wrong						43	17	16	16	8
I think euthanasia (mercy killing) is wrong	29	23	27	12	9	28	19	28	18	8
I am concerned that divorce is becoming too easy to obtain	17	34	35	11	3	21	40	22	14	3
I am concerned that pornography is too readily available						19	37	24	16	3
I am concerned about the amount of violence on television	6	20	27	35	12	6	27	24	37	6
I think parking restrictions should be strictly obeyed	14	42	30	11	3	10	48	25	13	3
There is nothing wrong in travelling without a ticket providing you are not caught	3	10	12	40	36	3	11	11	45	29
There is nothing wrong in selling cigarettes to children under the legal age	5	11	12	24	48	3	8	12	34	43

Table 7.1   Moral Attitudes (continued)

	13-15 year olds				16-20 year olds			
	AS%	A%	NC%	D%	DS%	AS%	A%	NC%	D%	DS%
I have never told a lie	1	2	3	40	54	0	1	2	40	57
I have never broken my promise	2	10	24	53	11	3	11	16	58	11
Sometimes I have taken advantage of people	10	58	19	11	2	9	60	18	10	2
I have never stolen anything in my life	23	13	14	36	14	15	12	12	49	12
Sometimes I have been jealous of others	18	68	8	5	1	20	69	4	5	1
Sometimes I feel resentful when I don't get my own way	7	60	18	12	3	5	57	16	20	2
I am always willing to admit when I make a mistake	9	37	25	27	2	9	43	19	27	2

Table 8.1   Politics and Society

	13-15 year olds					16-20 year olds				
	AS%	A%	NC%	D%	DS%	AS%	A%	NC%	D%	DS%
I have a lot of confidence in the policies of the Conservative party	7	10	38	19	26	5	13	37	20	26
I have a lot of confidence in the policies of the Labour party	5	7	38	20	29	5	12	36	24	24
I have a lot of confidence in the policies of the Liberal party	2	5	45	23	25	2	6	44	26	23
I have a lot of confidence in the policies of the National Front	1	2	33	22	42	1	1	16	20	63
Politics is important to me	3	13	31	30	23	9	25	27	27	12
I take an active part in politics	1	2	12	39	46	1	3	9	46	41
It makes no difference which political party is in power	6	24	28	26	16	5	16	25	33	21
I think the nationalisation of industry is a good thing	3	14	64	12	7	3	18	45	22	12
I think private medicine should be encouraged						6	18	42	21	12
I think private schools should be abolished						7	13	28	35	18
I think the trade unions have too much power	25	27	40	6	2	26	37	24	10	3
I think immigration into Britain should be restricted	18	35	28	13	7	17	44	20	14	5
There are too many black people living in this country	10	16	21	26	27	7	17	20	29	28
I would rather buy a British car than one made in another country	12	15	36	27	10	13	18	33	26	10
I am worried about the world situation	12	42	34	11	1	15	53	17	13	2

Table 8.1 Politics and Society (continued)

	13-15 year olds					16-20 year olds				
	AS%	A%	NC%	D%	DS%	AS%	A%	NC%	D%	DS%
I am concerned about the risk of nuclear war	37	32	21	8	2	31	41	13	11	4
I am concerned about the risk of pollution to the environment	21	42	26	8	3	19	50	20	10	1
I am concerned about people who are homeless	23	54	18	4	1	16	61	17	5	0
I am concerned about the poverty of the Third World	19	41	29	8	4	22	50	22	4	2
I am concerned about the rate of inflation	16	40	32	9	2	14	60	16	9	2
I am concerned about the problems of unemployment	19	49	23	6	2	23	60	12	6	0
Most unemployed people could have a job if they really wanted to	14	30	29	21	7	11	27	23	26	13
I am concerned with the rise in the crime rate	22	46	23	6	2	19	53	17	8	2
I am concerned that the health service is inefficient	7	20	35	31	7	9	34	22	31	4
There is nothing I can do to help solve the world's problems	6	19	33	29	12	3	17	31	37	12

Table 9.1 Work and Leisure

	13-15 year olds					16-20 year olds				
	AS%	A%	NC%	D%	DS%	AS%	A%	NC%	D%	DS%
I am happy in my work	37	49	9	3	2	42	43	8	5	2
I like the people I work with (go to school with)	46	46	5	2	1	43	50	5	1	1
I often worry about my work	12	45	14	22	7	11	36	14	32	7
I think it is important to work hard	42	52	5	1	0	35	59	4	2	0
I want to get to the top of my work	40	47	10	3	0	35	46	12	6	1
Spending money is important to me	13	33	23	26	5	10	34	17	34	5
I would rather go on social security than get a job I don't like doing	3	13	23	34	27	3	9	22	41	25
I often listen to music in my leisure time	39	46	5	8	2	42	48	3	6	1
I regularly listen to the radio or television news	35	50	7	6	1	44	48	3	5	0
I often read books in my leisure time	31	42	6	15	6	26	44	5	20	5
I take an active part in sport	35	34	11	14	5	25	35	7	24	9
I often watch sport in my leisure time	28	42	9	17	4	20	41	7	26	5
I often go drinking with my friends						12	33	8	33	14
I wish I had more things to do with my leisure time	18	32	11	25	13	9	27	7	38	19

Table 10.1 Well-being and Worry

	13-15 year olds					16-20 year olds				
	AS%	A%	NC%	D%	DS%	AS%	A%	NC%	D%	DS%
I find life really worth living	35	48	14	2	1	40	45	11	3	1
I feel my life has a sense of purpose	15	47	33	4	1	23	50	22	5	1
I often feel depressed						6	26	14	37	17
I have sometimes considered taking my own life						2	13	6	18	61
I am worried about my relationships with other people	11	22	25	29	13	12	22	17	33	16
I am worried about my sex life						2	7	17	44	30
I am worried that I cannot cope	5	16	25	35	19	4	12	16	42	26
I am worried about my health	10	15	15	37	24	3	12	14	43	28
I am worried that I might have a breakdown						1	5	8	36	50
My appearance is important to me	34	50	8	6	1	26	63	6	4	1
What people think of me is important	33	42	14	8	3	24	50	12	11	3
Friends are important to me	68	27	3	1	0	73	25	2	1	0
I tend to be a lonely person	4	10	16	44	25	3	18	11	47	21
I feel no one knows me	2	6	13	40	39	3	10	14	41	32
I like to have a lot of people around me	14	42	24	18	2	13	41	23	20	3

Table 10.1 Well-being and Worry (continued)

	13-15 year olds					16-20 year olds				
	AS%	A%	NC%	D%	DS%	AS%	A%	NC%	D%	DS%
I find crowds oppressive	3	19	40	29	10	4	19	25	43	9
I like to do things that are a little frightening	17	43	21	15	4	9	40	28	21	3
I feel I am not worth much as a person		23	24	32	13	3	9	17	40	32
I often long for someone to turn to for advice	8	23	15	13	5	6	24	15	41	14
I have found it helpful to talk about my problems with my mother	25	42	15	13	5	20	41	14	17	8
I have found it helpful to talk about my problems with my father	5	23	23	32	17	5	24	17	32	22
I have found it helpful to talk about my problems with close friends	23	36	19	15	6	30	44	13	10	3
I have found it helpful to talk about my problems with a minister of religion	1	13	33	35	18	4	18	24	38	16
I would never discuss my problems with a minister of religion	12	22	39	20	6	9	18	29	32	12